RIRI WILLIAMS
IRONHEART
THOSE WITH COURAGE

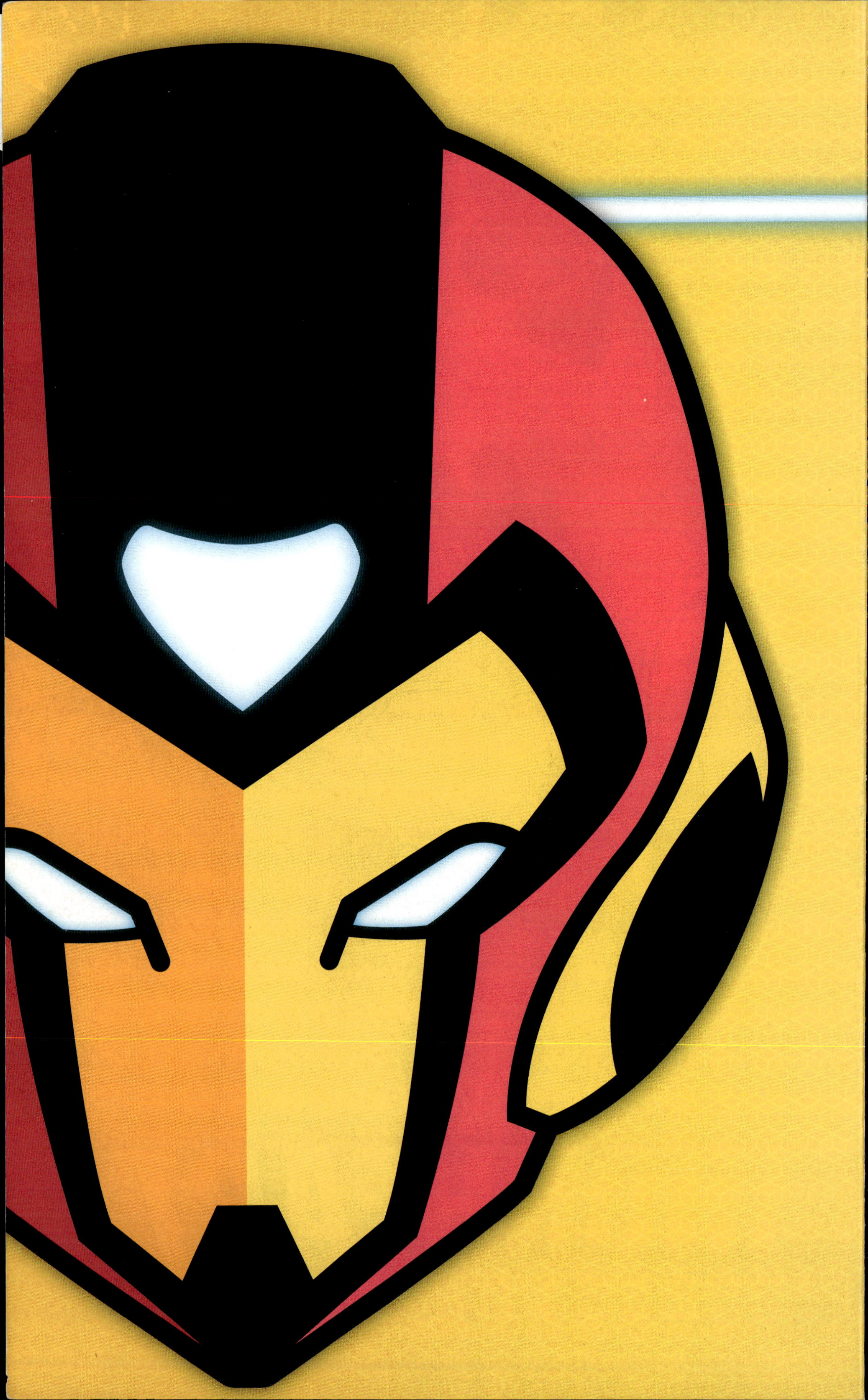

Riri Williams was a young girl who dreamed of becoming an astronaut--until her best friend and stepfather were killed in a drive-by shooting. Determined to find a way to protect her hometown of Chicago, Riri reverse engineered Tony Stark's Iron Man design to create her own armor. Now she soars the skies as...

RIRI WILLIAMS IRONHEART
THOSE WITH COURAGE

EVE L. EWING
WRITER

LUCIANO VECCHIO (#1-5) &
KEVIN LIBRANDA (#1, #6)
ARTISTS

GEOFFO
ADDITIONAL LAYOUTS

MATT MILLA
COLOR ARTIST

VC's CLAYTON COWLES
LETTERER

AMY REEDER
COVER ART

SHANNON ANDREWS
ASSISTANT EDITOR

ALANNA SMITH & **TOM BREVOORT**
EDITORS

COLLECTION EDITOR **JENNIFER GRÜNWALD**
ASSISTANT EDITOR **CAITLIN O'CONNELL**
ASSOCIATE MANAGING EDITOR **KATERI WOODY**
EDITOR, SPECIAL PROJECTS **MARK D. BEAZLEY**
VP PRODUCTION & SPECIAL PROJECTS **JEFF YOUNGQUIST**
BOOK DESIGNER **ADAM DEL RE**

SVP PRINT, SALES & MARKETING **DAVID GABRIEL**
DIRECTOR, LICENSED PUBLISHING **SVEN LARSEN**
EDITOR IN CHIEF **C.B. CEBULSKI**
CHIEF CREATIVE OFFICER **JOE QUESADA**
PRESIDENT **DAN BUCKLEY**
EXECUTIVE PRODUCER **ALAN FINE**

IRONHEART VOL. 1: THOSE WITH COURAGE. Contains material originally published in magazine form as IRONHEART #1-6. First printing 2019. ISBN 978-1-302-91508-7. Published by MARVEL WORLDWIDE, INC., a subsidiary of MARVEL ENTERTAINMENT, LLC. OFFICE OF PUBLICATION: 135 West 50th Street, New York, NY 10020. © 2019 MARVEL No similarity between any of the names, characters, persons, and/or institutions in this magazine with those of any living or dead person or institution is intended, and any such similarity which may exist is purely coincidental. **Printed in the U.S.A.** DAN BUCKLEY, President, Marvel Entertainment; JOHN NEE, Publisher; JOE QUESADA, Chief Creative Officer; TOM BREVOORT, SVP of Publishing; DAVID BOGART, Associate Publisher & SVP of Talent Affairs; DAVID GABRIEL, SVP of Sales & Marketing, Publishing; JEFF YOUNGQUIST, VP of Production & Special Projects; DAN CARR, Executive Director of Publishing Technology; ALEX MORALES, Director of Publishing Operations; DAN EDINGTON, Managing Editor; SUSAN CRESPI, Production Manager; STAN LEE, Chairman Emeritus. For information regarding advertising in Marvel Comics or on Marvel.com, please contact Vit DeBellis, Custom Solutions & Integrated Advertising Manager, at vdebellis@marvel.com. For Marvel subscription inquiries, please call 888-511-5480. **Manufactured between 5/17/2019 and 6/18/2019 by LSC COMMUNICATIONS INC., KENDALLVILLE, IN, USA.**

10 9 8 7 6 5 4 3 2 1

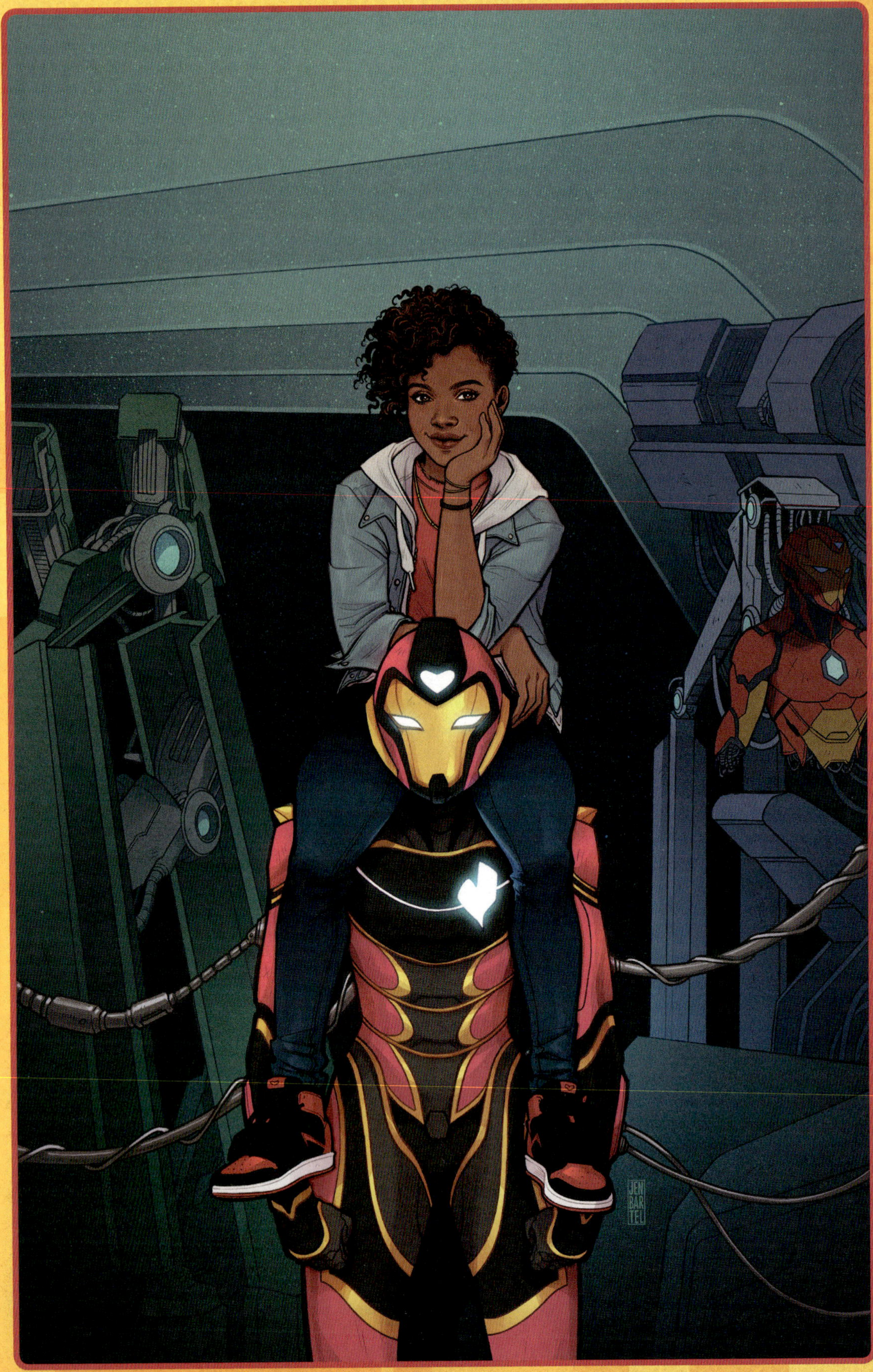
JEN
BAR
TEL

JEN BARTEL
#1 VARIANT

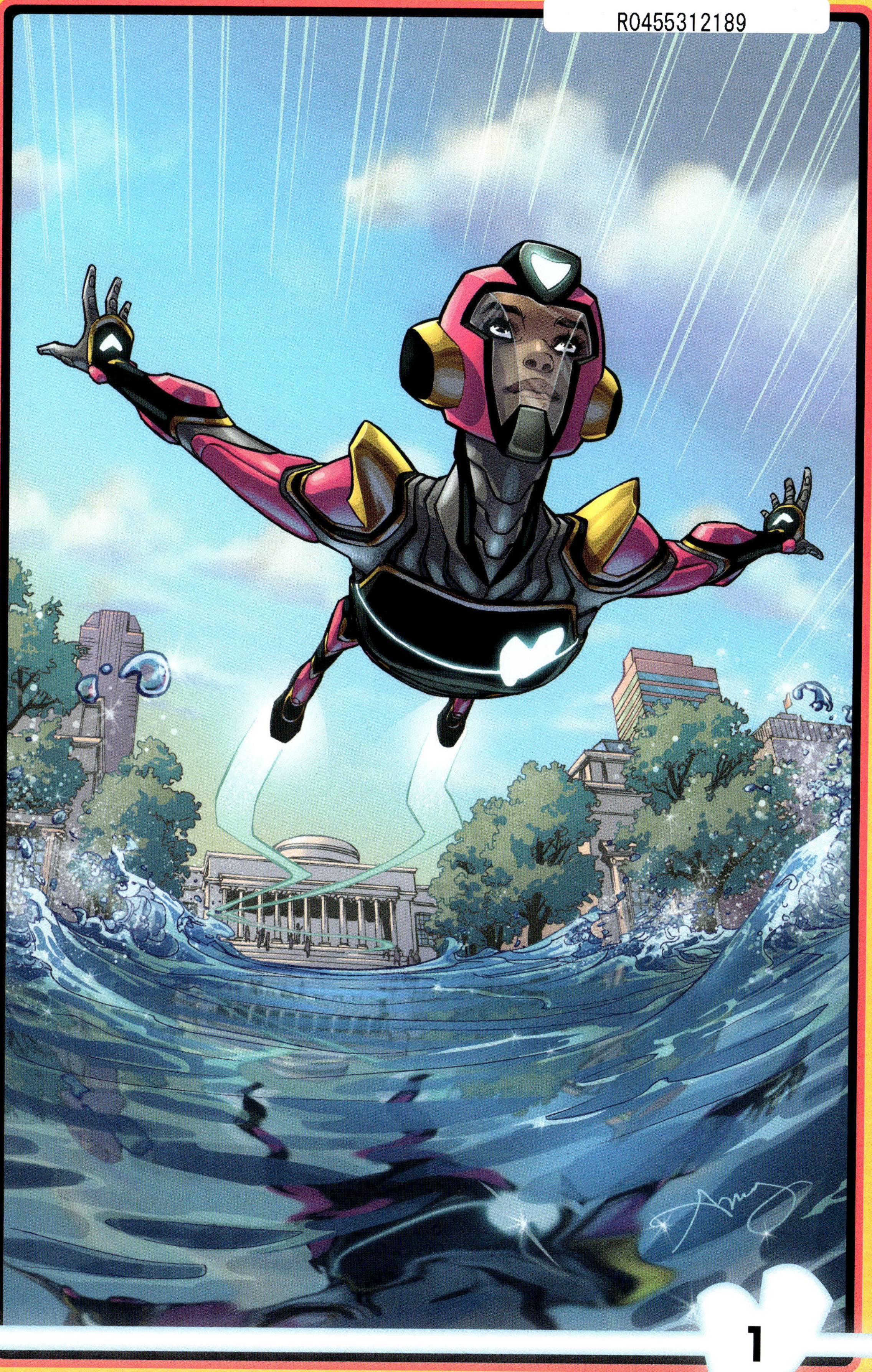

1

I WAS NEVER MEANT TO FLY.

SO MUCH HAS CHANGED IN MY LIFE, SO QUICKLY. HOW DID I GO FROM BEING A NO-NAME BLACK GIRL MESSING AROUND ALONE IN MY GARAGE IN CHICAGO TO BEING...A SUPER HERO?

AND YEAH, I GET IT. EVERY SUPER HERO HAS THEIR GOLLY-GEE, MILD-MANNERED, HUMBLE ORIGIN STORY.

BUT COMING FROM WHERE I COME FROM, I REALLY MEAN IT. I SHOULDN'T BE HERE.

MY FATHER--DEAD BEFORE I WAS BORN. MY STEPDAD, WHO RAISED ME--SHOT AND KILLED. NATALIE, WHO WAS MY UNDISPUTED BEST FRIEND BY VIRTUE OF BEING MY ONLY FRIEND--SHOT AND KILLED.

BUT HOW DOES THE POEM GO? "INTO A DAYBREAK THAT'S WONDROUSLY CLEAR...

"...I RISE."

WHAT DID I DO TO DESERVE TO LIVE WHEN THEY DIDN'T? WHAT DID I DO TO DESERVE TO FLY?

THESE DAYS I SPEND SO MUCH TIME UP HERE, ALONE, HOPING TO FIGURE THAT OUT. HONESTLY, I COULD STAY UP HERE ALL DAY.

BUT NO MATTER HOW GOOD IT FEELS TO KEEP MY HEAD IN THE CLOUDS, EVENTUALLY, I HAVE TO COME RIGHT BACK DOWN TO EARTH.

MASSACHUSETTS INSTITUTE OF TECHNOLOGY.

WELL, LOOK WHO'S DECIDED TO JOIN US.
DEAN BRYANT. I DIDN'T EXPECT TO SEE YOU HERE.
WITH GUESTS. HI. WHO ARE YOU AND WHAT ARE YOU DOING IN MY LAB?
AHEM. EVERYONE, THAT'S THAT YOUTHFUL ENERGY I WAS TELLING YOU ABOUT. PLEASE PARDON MS. WILLIAMS.
RIRI, THIS IS AN ESTEEMED DELEGATION OF WORLD LEADERS, ALL VISITING CAMBRIDGE FOR THE GLOBAL SUMMIT TAKING PLACE LATER TODAY. I'M SURE YOU'VE SEEN IT ALL OVER THE NEWS.
THESE VERY IMPORTANT PEOPLE CAME HERE TO GET A SNEAK PEEK AT YOUR LAB AND I TOLD THEM YOU WOULD BE OVERJOYED TO GIVE THEM A LITTLE TOUR.
OKAY, I HEAR YOU LOUD AND CLEAR.
UH, HI, EVERYONE. I'M--I'M SORRY, I DON'T SPEAK A SECOND LANGUAGE. IS THERE A TRANSLATOR OR SOMETHING?
NO WORRIES, MS. WILLIAMS. WE'RE EQUIPPED WITH PORTABLE TRANSLATORS THAT TAKE IN YOUR LANGUAGE, PROVIDE AUDIO TRANSLATION IN OUR EARPIECES AND INSTANTLY TRANSLATE OUR RESPONSES TO YOU.
I AM SPEAKING TWI RIGHT NOW, AND YOU ARE HEARING ME IN ENGLISH.

Panel 1:
THAT'S... ACTUALLY, THAT'S PRETTY COOL.
OKAY, WELL, WELCOME TO MY LAB. I'LL SHOW YOU A COUPLE THINGS IN DEVELOPMENT. UMMM...

Panel 2:
WELL...

Panel 3:
I'M WORKING ON A VISOR THAT INCORPORATES MICROSCOPIC-SCALE ANALYSIS FOR IMPROVED FORENSIC DATA INTAKE IN THE FIELD.
WITH THIS BABY, YOU CAN SEE BLOOD AND SKIN REMNANTS LEFT ON A SURFACE AT A *CELLULAR LEVEL*. TRY IT.

Panel 4:
GOOD GOD! YOUR SKIN! EVERYTHING IN THIS ROOM! IT'S CRAWLING WITH BUGS AND VERMIN! IT'S *WRETCHED*!
YEAH, SORRY, I GUESS IT'S KINDA GROSS TO LIVE IN THE MICROSCOPIC WORLD.
WELL, I ALSO HAVE...

Panel 5:
...THIS PLATE FROM AN EXPERIMENTAL SUIT RETROFIT THAT WOULD BE CAPABLE OF WITHSTANDING VIRTUALLY INFINITE PRESSURE!
YOU COULD JOURNEY TO THE CENTER OF THE OCEAN WITHOUT YOUR RIB CAGE COLLAPSING LIKE A USED PIECE OF *ALUMINUM FOIL* AND EVERY TISSUE IN YOUR *BODY* BEING REDUCED TO A *SHREDDED*, UNRECOGNIZABLE PIECE OF--

UHHHHH... SORRY ABOUT THE GRAPHIC IMAGERY.
AHEM. ANYTHING ELSE, MS. WILLIAMS?
AND, UM, THIS IS AN ARM CANNON THAT'S ALSO A 3D PRINTER.
AND IT GLOWS IN THE DARK.
OOOOH!
LET ME SEE!
MS. WILLIAMS, YOU'RE QUITE THE ENGINEER. IS THIS A LIFELONG INTEREST? PERHAPS AS A CHILD YOU ENJOYED TINKERING IN THE GARAGE WITH YOUR FATHER?
MY FATHER IS DEAD, SO NO. LIFELONG INTEREST, YES. NEXT QUESTION.
I DID READ THAT ABOUT YOU--YOUR FATHER WAS SHOT AND KILLED. AND YOUR BEST FRIEND. AND YET IRONHEART, MUCH LIKE IRON MAN, IS A WEAPON. DO YOU--
IRONHEART IS NOT A WEAPON. IRONHEART IS AN ENGINEER WHO USES MANY TOOLS. INCLUDING FORCE, SOMETIMES. BUT I TRY TO AVOID THAT.
WHAT KIND OF A.I. DOES THE SUIT HAVE? DOES IT HAVE A PERSONALITY, LIKE TONY STARK'S FAMOUS FRIDAY?
OH! FUNNY YOU SHOULD ASK. RIGHT NOW, NO. BUT THAT'S SOMETHING I'VE BEEN WORKING ON. I'M RUNNING ANALYTICS ON MY OWN BEHAVIORS, WEAKNESSES, EVEN MY DREAMS! I WANT TO SYNTHESIZE AN A.I. SYSTEM THAT WILL SERVE AS AN EFFECTIVE COMPLEMENT TO--

WHOA!
I GOT IT!
WHAT ON EARTH WAS THAT ALL ABOUT?! THAT THING JUST... JUST... SOMEONE COULD HAVE BEEN *KILLED!*
SORRY, EVERYONE. I DON'T KNOW WHAT COULD HAVE SET IT OFF. NOTHING LIKE THAT HAS EVER HAPPENED BEFORE.
MS. WILLIAMS, IF YOU CAN'T ADDRESS BASIC SAFETY CONCERNS, PERHAPS YOU SHOULDN'T BE RUNNING YOUR OWN LAB AFTER ALL.
WELL, MAYBE IF YOU DIDN'T TREAT THIS WORKSPACE LIKE A *ZOO* WHERE YOU CAN DROP BY WHENEVER YOU WANT WITH A LITTLE *FIELD TRIP*, THERE WOULDN'T *BE* ANY SAFETY CONCERNS!
CAN WE GO?
YES, I BELIEVE WE'RE BEHIND SCHEDULE. MY APOLOGIES.
WE'LL DISCUSS THIS *LATER*, MS. WILLIAMS.
BYE! THANKS FOR VISITING! HAVE FUN TALKING ABOUT HOW TO FIX THE WORLD AND STUFF!
...AND PLEASE NEVER COME BACK TO MY LAB BECAUSE I HAVE NO IDEA WHAT JUST HAPPENED.
TAKE CARE NOW!

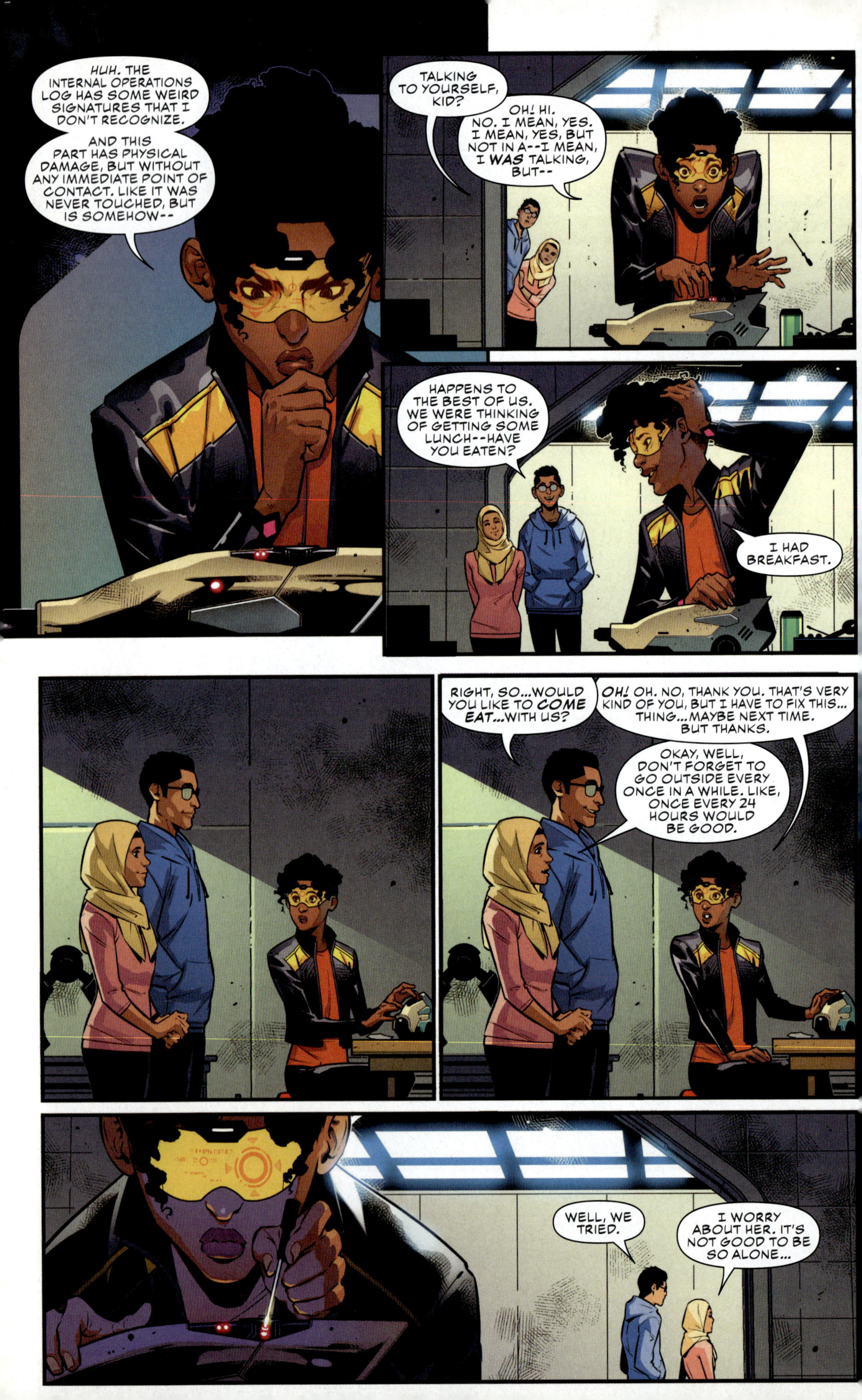

HUH. THE INTERNAL OPERATIONS LOG HAS SOME WEIRD SIGNATURES THAT I DON'T RECOGNIZE.
AND THIS PART HAS PHYSICAL DAMAGE, BUT WITHOUT ANY IMMEDIATE POINT OF CONTACT. LIKE IT WAS NEVER TOUCHED, BUT IS SOMEHOW--
TALKING TO YOURSELF, KID?
OH! HI. NO. I MEAN, YES. I MEAN, YES, BUT NOT IN A--I MEAN, I WAS TALKING, BUT--
HAPPENS TO THE BEST OF US. WE WERE THINKING OF GETTING SOME LUNCH--HAVE YOU EATEN?
I HAD BREAKFAST.
RIGHT, SO...WOULD YOU LIKE TO COME EAT...WITH US?
OH! OH. NO, THANK YOU. THAT'S VERY KIND OF YOU, BUT I HAVE TO FIX THIS... THING...MAYBE NEXT TIME. BUT THANKS.
OKAY, WELL, DON'T FORGET TO GO OUTSIDE EVERY ONCE IN A WHILE. LIKE, ONCE EVERY 24 HOURS WOULD BE GOOD.
WELL, WE TRIED.
I WORRY ABOUT HER. IT'S NOT GOOD TO BE SO ALONE...

WE'RE HERE AT THE KENNEDY SCHOOL OF GOVERNMENT AT HARVARD UNIVERSITY, WHERE THE WORLD LEADERS GATHERED FOR TODAY'S SUMMIT HAVE JUST ABOUT FINISHED FILING INTO THE BUILDING.
AS YOU CAN SEE, ROBIN, THE AREA IS SUBJECT TO HEIGHTENED SECURITY MEASURES.
A SOURCE TELLS US THAT THE PROTOCOLS AND EQUIPMENT COME FROM PARKER INDUSTRIES, WHICH OF COURSE IMPLODED LAST YEAR, BUT IS STILL CONSIDERED TO HAVE BEEN A GLOBAL LEADER IN CUTTING-EDGE SECURITY TECH. WE ALSO KNOW--
TV3
WHAT'S HAPPENING?
OH MY GOD, I CAN'T MOVE!
HELP!
MY CAMERA JUST STOPPED WORKING!
MINE TOO!
THE DIPLOMATS ARE ALL INSIDE THE BUILDING! GET TO THEM IMMEDIATELY! CODE DOUBLE-RED! IMPLEMENT THE PROTOCOL!
WE CAN'T GET THROUGH, CAPTAIN!
WHAT DO YOU MEAN, YOU CAN'T GET THROUGH?!
IT'S LIKE THERE'S...SOME SORT OF WALL BLOCKING US!
THE NOISE! THAT HORRIBLE NOISE!

A-LERT. A-LERT. UNUSUAL POLICE ACTIVITY DETECTED IN PROXIMITY.
MAN, I NEED TO HURRY UP AND GET A REAL A.I.--THAT DISEMBODIED HAL VOICE IS WACK.
THANK YOU, COMPUTER. CAN YOU PLEASE CALL UP ANY RELEVANT NEWS FOOTAGE FROM THE LAST FEW MINUTES?
T-V3
--GLOBAL SUMMIT IN UTTER CHAOS. RUMORS THAT THE NATIONAL GUARD--
OH BOY. WELL, BROKEN ARM CANNON, YOU'LL HAVE TO WAIT.
I NEED TO RUN DOWN THE STREET FOR A SECOND...
...AND THEN AFTER THIS, I REALLY DO NEED TO GET LUNCH.

WHAT IS HAPPENING OUT THERE?
EVERYTHING WILL BE FINE, YOUR EXCELLENCY. WE JUST NEED YOU TO SHELTER IN PLACE.
YOU MEAN THAT WHILE THIS SUPPOSED TOP-NOTCH SECURITY DETAIL IS OUTSIDE SCREAMING THEIR HEADS OFF, YOU WANT US TO HIDE UNDER THE TABLE.
IT'S FOR YOUR OWN SAFETY, YOUR EXCELLENCY.
OH, I THINK YOU ARE QUITE RIGHT TO BE DUBIOUS, PRIME MINISTER.
THESE MEN CAN'T PROTECT YOU.
POLICE

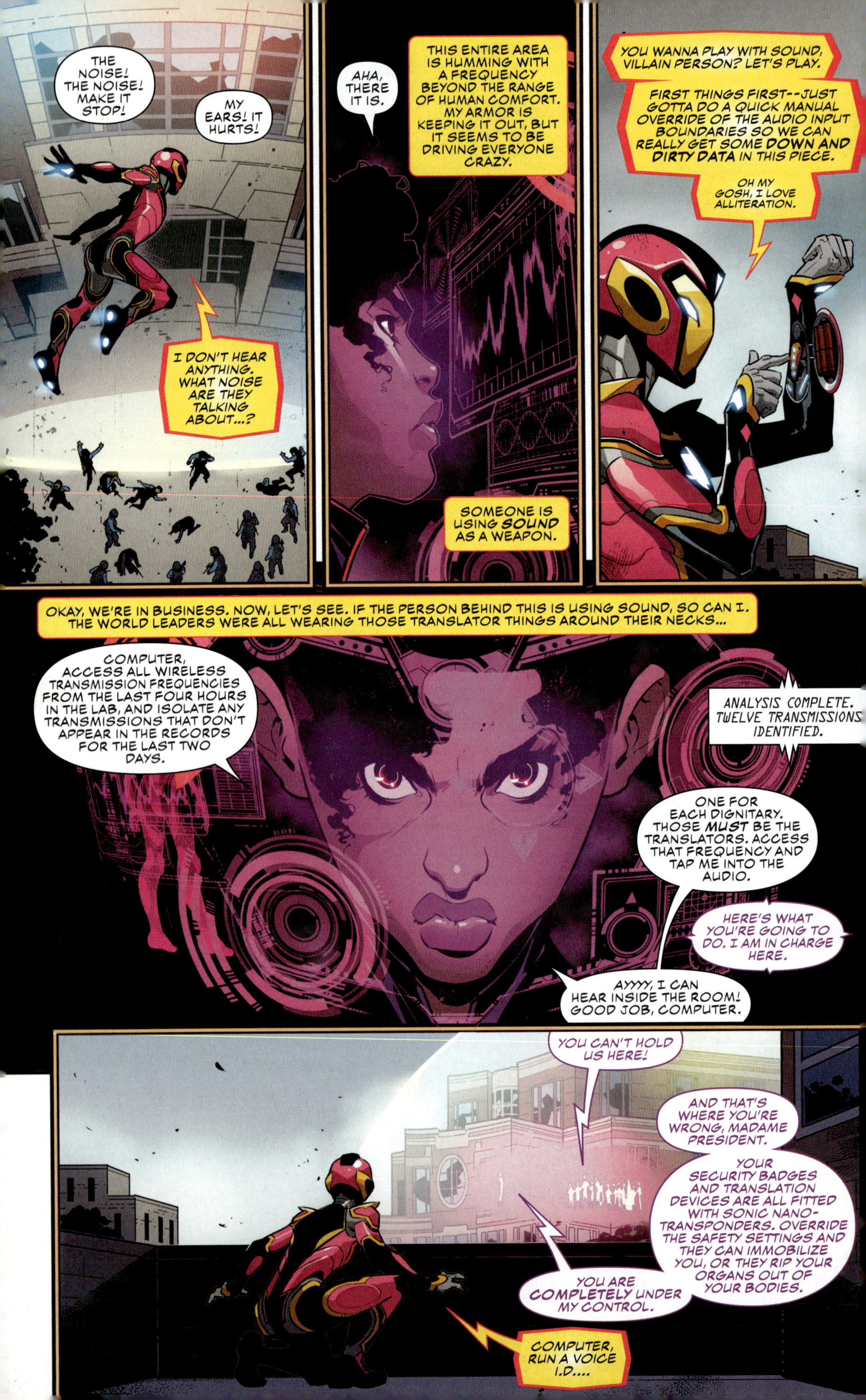

THE NOISE! THE NOISE! MAKE IT STOP!
MY EARS! IT HURTS!
I DON'T HEAR ANYTHING. WHAT NOISE ARE THEY TALKING ABOUT...?
AHA, THERE IT IS.
THIS ENTIRE AREA IS HUMMING WITH A FREQUENCY BEYOND THE RANGE OF HUMAN COMFORT. MY ARMOR IS KEEPING IT OUT, BUT IT SEEMS TO BE DRIVING EVERYONE CRAZY.
SOMEONE IS USING SOUND AS A WEAPON.
YOU WANNA PLAY WITH SOUND, VILLAIN PERSON? LET'S PLAY.
FIRST THINGS FIRST--JUST GOTTA DO A QUICK MANUAL OVERRIDE OF THE AUDIO INPUT BOUNDARIES SO WE CAN REALLY GET SOME DOWN AND DIRTY DATA IN THIS PIECE.
OH MY GOSH, I LOVE ALLITERATION.
OKAY, WE'RE IN BUSINESS. NOW, LET'S SEE. IF THE PERSON BEHIND THIS IS USING SOUND, SO CAN I. THE WORLD LEADERS WERE ALL WEARING THOSE TRANSLATOR THINGS AROUND THEIR NECKS...
COMPUTER, ACCESS ALL WIRELESS TRANSMISSION FREQUENCIES FROM THE LAST FOUR HOURS IN THE LAB, AND ISOLATE ANY TRANSMISSIONS THAT DON'T APPEAR IN THE RECORDS FOR THE LAST TWO DAYS.
ANALYSIS COMPLETE. TWELVE TRANSMISSIONS IDENTIFIED.
ONE FOR EACH DIGNITARY. THOSE MUST BE THE TRANSLATORS. ACCESS THAT FREQUENCY AND TAP ME INTO THE AUDIO.
HERE'S WHAT YOU'RE GOING TO DO. I AM IN CHARGE HERE.
AYYYY, I CAN HEAR INSIDE THE ROOM! GOOD JOB, COMPUTER.
YOU CAN'T HOLD US HERE!
AND THAT'S WHERE YOU'RE WRONG, MADAME PRESIDENT.
YOUR SECURITY BADGES AND TRANSLATION DEVICES ARE ALL FITTED WITH SONIC NANO-TRANSPONDERS. OVERRIDE THE SAFETY SETTINGS AND THEY CAN IMMOBILIZE YOU, OR THEY RIP YOUR ORGANS OUT OF YOUR BODIES.
YOU ARE COMPLETELY UNDER MY CONTROL.
COMPUTER, RUN A VOICE I.D....

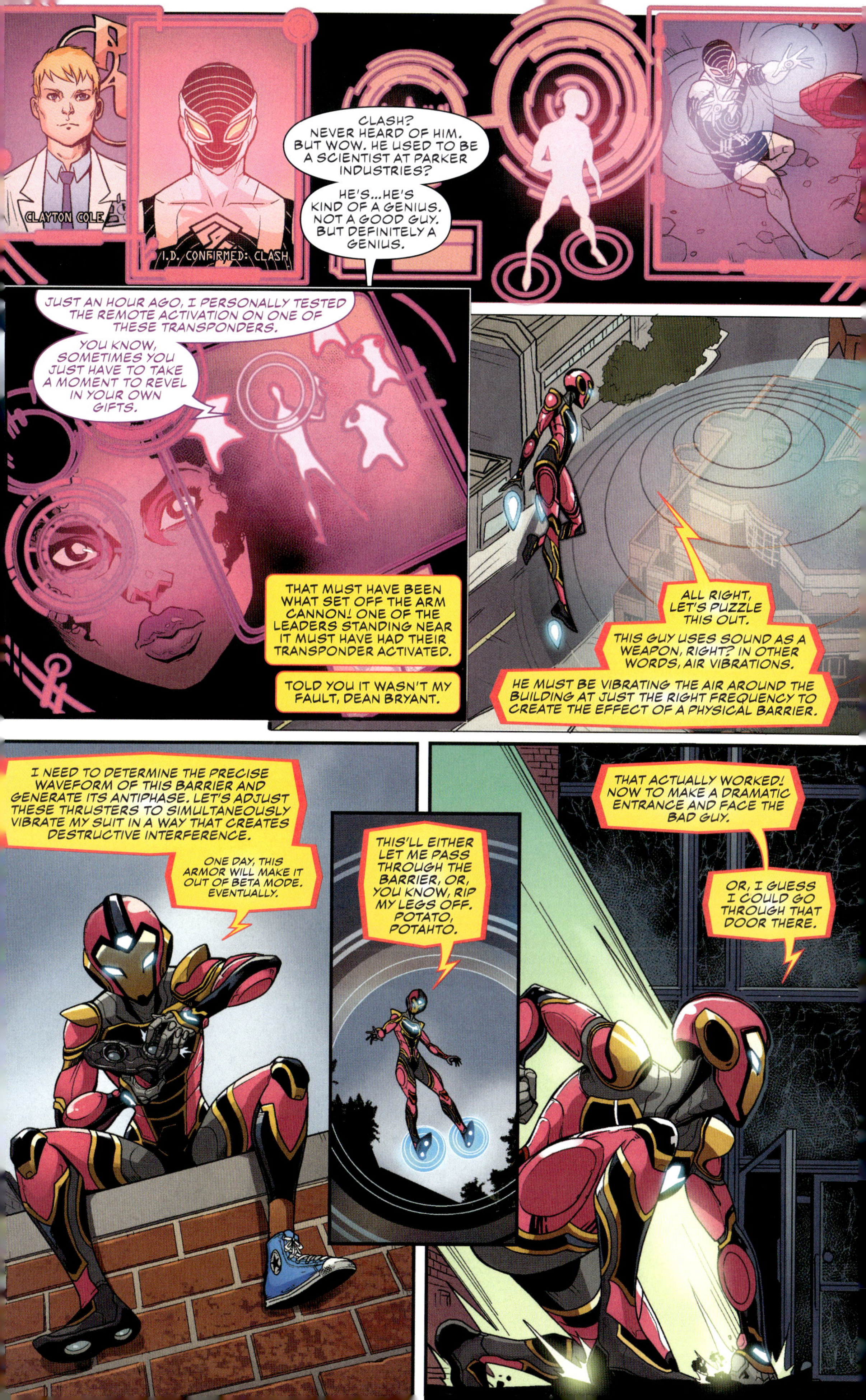

CLAYTON COLE
I.D. CONFIRMED: CLASH
CLASH? NEVER HEARD OF HIM. BUT WOW. HE USED TO BE A SCIENTIST AT PARKER INDUSTRIES?
HE'S...HE'S KIND OF A GENIUS. NOT A GOOD GUY. BUT DEFINITELY A GENIUS.
JUST AN HOUR AGO, I PERSONALLY TESTED THE REMOTE ACTIVATION ON ONE OF THESE TRANSPONDERS.
YOU KNOW, SOMETIMES YOU JUST HAVE TO TAKE A MOMENT TO REVEL IN YOUR OWN GIFTS.
THAT MUST HAVE BEEN WHAT SET OFF THE ARM CANNON! ONE OF THE LEADERS STANDING NEAR IT MUST HAVE HAD THEIR TRANSPONDER ACTIVATED.
TOLD YOU IT WASN'T MY FAULT, DEAN BRYANT.
ALL RIGHT, LET'S PUZZLE THIS OUT.
THIS GUY USES SOUND AS A WEAPON, RIGHT? IN OTHER WORDS, AIR VIBRATIONS.
HE MUST BE VIBRATING THE AIR AROUND THE BUILDING AT JUST THE RIGHT FREQUENCY TO CREATE THE EFFECT OF A PHYSICAL BARRIER.
I NEED TO DETERMINE THE PRECISE WAVEFORM OF THIS BARRIER AND GENERATE ITS ANTIPHASE. LET'S ADJUST THESE THRUSTERS TO SIMULTANEOUSLY VIBRATE MY SUIT IN A WAY THAT CREATES DESTRUCTIVE INTERFERENCE.
ONE DAY, THIS ARMOR WILL MAKE IT OUT OF BETA MODE. EVENTUALLY.
THIS'LL EITHER LET ME PASS THROUGH THE BARRIER, OR, YOU KNOW, RIP MY LEGS OFF. POTATO, POTAHTO.
THAT ACTUALLY WORKED! NOW TO MAKE A DRAMATIC ENTRANCE AND FACE THE BAD GUY.
OR, I GUESS I COULD GO THROUGH THAT DOOR THERE.

ARE YOU GOING TO KILL US?

WHAT IS THE TEN RINGS?

NOTHING BUT SENSELESS TALES. AND THIS MADMAN DOESN'T BEAR THEIR INSIGNIA.

DO NOT FEAR, YOUR EXCELLENCY. I WOULD NEVER SEEK TO KILL YOU WHEN I CAN *CONTROL* YOU.

AND *CONTROL* IS WHAT THE *TEN RINGS* SEEKS ABOVE ALL.

WHAT'S THAT OLD SAYING? "DRESS FOR THE JOB YOU WANT"?

SO I'M...TAKING *HOSTAGES* FOR THE JOB I WANT.

WHAT BETTER WAY TO CONVINCE THE TEN RINGS THAT I DESERVE TO JOIN THEIR ESTEEMED RANKS THAN BY *PROVING* IT?

BY SHOWING THEM THAT I'M MORE THAN A JOKE, MORE THAN SOMEONE TO BE DISRESPECTED.

SOMEONE TO BE WALKED ON, LIKE A *NOBODY*.

SO YOU ADMIT IT. YOU'RE NOTHING BUT A WORTHLESS IMITATOR.

THE ONLY THING MORE PATHETIC THAN A VIOLENT TERRORIST IS SOMEONE *PRETENDING* TO BE ONE.

I *TRIED*, YOUR EXCELLENCY. I TRIED KINDNESS. I TRIED *REDEMPTION*. AND YOU KNOW WHAT BECAME CLEAR OVER AND OVER? THAT THERE IS NO SUCH THING. THIS WORLD IS FULL OF HYPOCRITES AND SINNERS.

THE PETER PARKERS AND STEVE ROGERSES OF THE WORLD FEEL LIKE THEY CAN JUDGE PEOPLE. EVEN MY OWN PARENTS STILL SAW ME AS A MONSTER.

SO YES. I'M A VIOLENT TERRORIST. A VERY *REAL* ONE. I INTEND TO MAKE THAT CLEAR TODAY.

EACH OF YOU IS GOING TO SIT HERE AND BROKER THE DEALS I DEMAND FROM YOU. FROM SOME OF YOU, I WANT ARMS. FROM OTHERS, I WANT SECRETS. AND SOME OF YOU... WELL, YOU MAY BE MORE VALUABLE TO ME *DEAD*.

HEY!

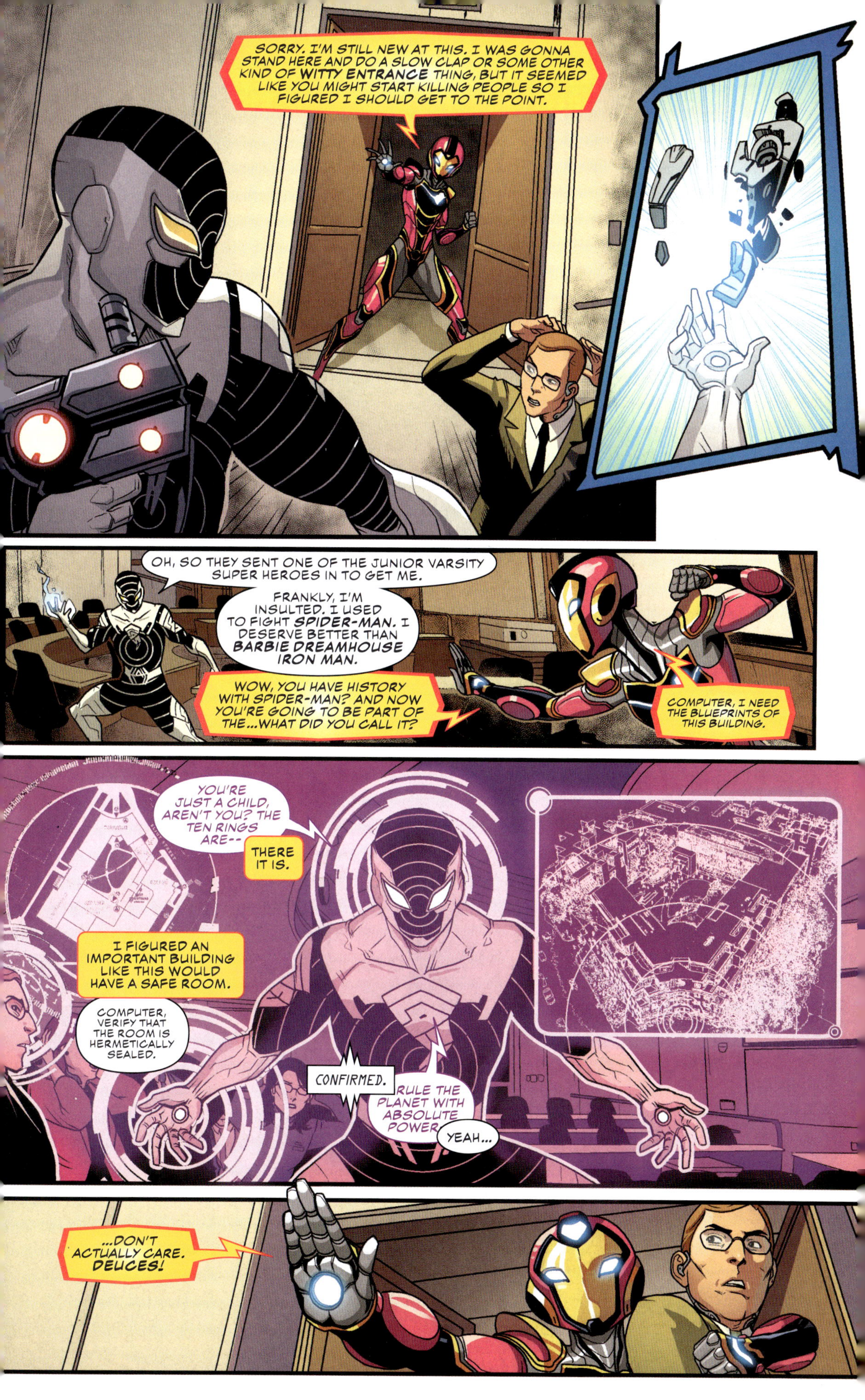
SORRY. I'M STILL NEW AT THIS. I WAS GONNA STAND HERE AND DO A SLOW CLAP OR SOME OTHER KIND OF WITTY ENTRANCE THING, BUT IT SEEMED LIKE YOU MIGHT START KILLING PEOPLE SO I FIGURED I SHOULD GET TO THE POINT.
OH, SO THEY SENT ONE OF THE JUNIOR VARSITY SUPER HEROES IN TO GET ME.
FRANKLY, I'M INSULTED. I USED TO FIGHT SPIDER-MAN. I DESERVE BETTER THAN BARBIE DREAMHOUSE IRON MAN.
WOW, YOU HAVE HISTORY WITH SPIDER-MAN? AND NOW YOU'RE GOING TO BE PART OF THE...WHAT DID YOU CALL IT?
COMPUTER, I NEED THE BLUEPRINTS OF THIS BUILDING.
YOU'RE JUST A CHILD, AREN'T YOU? THE TEN RINGS ARE--
THERE IT IS.
I FIGURED AN IMPORTANT BUILDING LIKE THIS WOULD HAVE A SAFE ROOM.
COMPUTER, VERIFY THAT THE ROOM IS HERMETICALLY SEALED.
CONFIRMED.
RULE THE PLANET WITH ABSOLUTE POWER.
YEAH...
...DON'T ACTUALLY CARE. DEUCES!

QUICK. YOU MUST HAVE GOTTEN A SECURITY BRIEFING HERE, RIGHT? YOU'VE GOT CLEARANCE?! RETINAL SCANNER!
HUH?
YOUR EYEBALL!
WELCOME, GENERAL. SAFE ROOM ACCESS GRANTED. LOCAL AUTHORITIES AND FIRST RESPONDERS HAVE BEEN ALERTED.
OH, THEY HAVE? GREAT, WE'RE ALL SAVED.
OKAY, JUST STAY CALM. HE'LL BE HERE ANY--

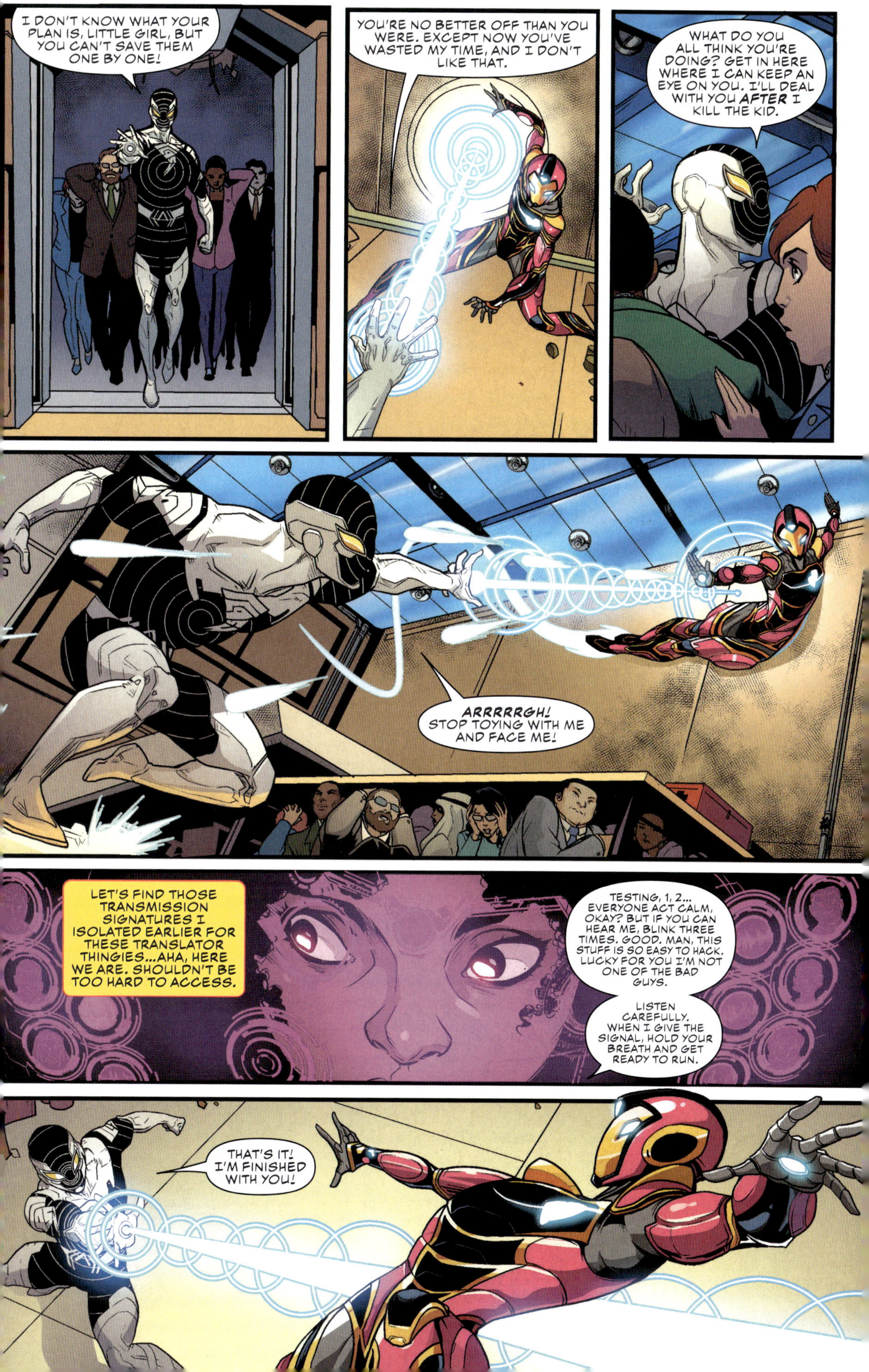
I DON'T KNOW WHAT YOUR PLAN IS, LITTLE GIRL, BUT YOU CAN'T SAVE THEM ONE BY ONE!
YOU'RE NO BETTER OFF THAN YOU WERE. EXCEPT NOW YOU'VE WASTED MY TIME, AND I DON'T LIKE THAT.
WHAT DO YOU ALL THINK YOU'RE DOING? GET IN HERE WHERE I CAN KEEP AN EYE ON YOU. I'LL DEAL WITH YOU AFTER I KILL THE KID.
ARRRRRGH! STOP TOYING WITH ME AND FACE ME!
LET'S FIND THOSE TRANSMISSION SIGNATURES I ISOLATED EARLIER FOR THESE TRANSLATOR THINGIES...AHA, HERE WE ARE. SHOULDN'T BE TOO HARD TO ACCESS.
TESTING, 1, 2... EVERYONE ACT CALM, OKAY? BUT IF YOU CAN HEAR ME, BLINK THREE TIMES. GOOD. MAN, THIS STUFF IS SO EASY TO HACK. LUCKY FOR YOU I'M NOT ONE OF THE BAD GUYS.
LISTEN CAREFULLY. WHEN I GIVE THE SIGNAL, HOLD YOUR BREATH AND GET READY TO RUN.
THAT'S IT! I'M FINISHED WITH YOU!

TRUST ME, SAME.
NOW!
STAY UNDER THE WATER AND TAKE THE HEADGEAR OFF!
THEIR CONTROLLING SOUNDWAVE FREQUENCIES WERE DESIGNED WITH AIR IN MIND--THEY WON'T WORK CORRECTLY UNDERWATER!
NOW RUN! YOU WON'T BE ABLE TO GET PAST CLASH'S BARRIER, BUT GET OUT OF THE BUILDING!

IMPRESSIVE, IRON GIRL. I HAVE TO ADMIT--TRULY IMPRESSIVE.
IT'S IRONHEART, BRO.
YOU THINK I CARE IF YOU DESTROY MY EQUIPMENT? THE WORLD LEADERS ARE STILL TRAPPED HERE.
MY BARRIER WILL HAVE THEM LYING ON THE GROUND SCREAMING LIKE THE REST OF THOSE FOOLS.
YOU KNOW WHAT? GOOD POINT.
HEY, YOU USING THE **LOCAL POWER GRID** TO OPERATE THOSE TRANSPONDERS YOU MUST HAVE BURIED BENEATH THE PERIMETER OF THIS BUILDING?
BECAUSE...
NO!

A BLACKOUT! THE BARRIER IS DOWN!
HELP US! GO GET HIM, HE'S IN THERE!
LET'S GO!
ENGAGE NIGHT VISION.
THE DARKNESS WON'T STOP ME, STUPID.
YOU'RE INTO SCIENCE-- EVER HEARD OF ECHOLOCATION?
EVER HEARD OF...MY SEMIAUTONOMOUS ELECTROMAGNETIC POWER MICRONODES? THAT'S RIGHT, YOU HAVEN'T!
I HAVEN'T PATENTED THEM YET BECAUSE THE NAME ISN'T VERY GOOD! THEY'RE PORTABLY SIZED AND THEY USE AN ELECTROMAGNETIC CURRENT TO--
OH, THE FIGHT IS OVER, HUH?
WELL, UM...YEAH, YOU LOST! KICK ROCKS, CLASH!

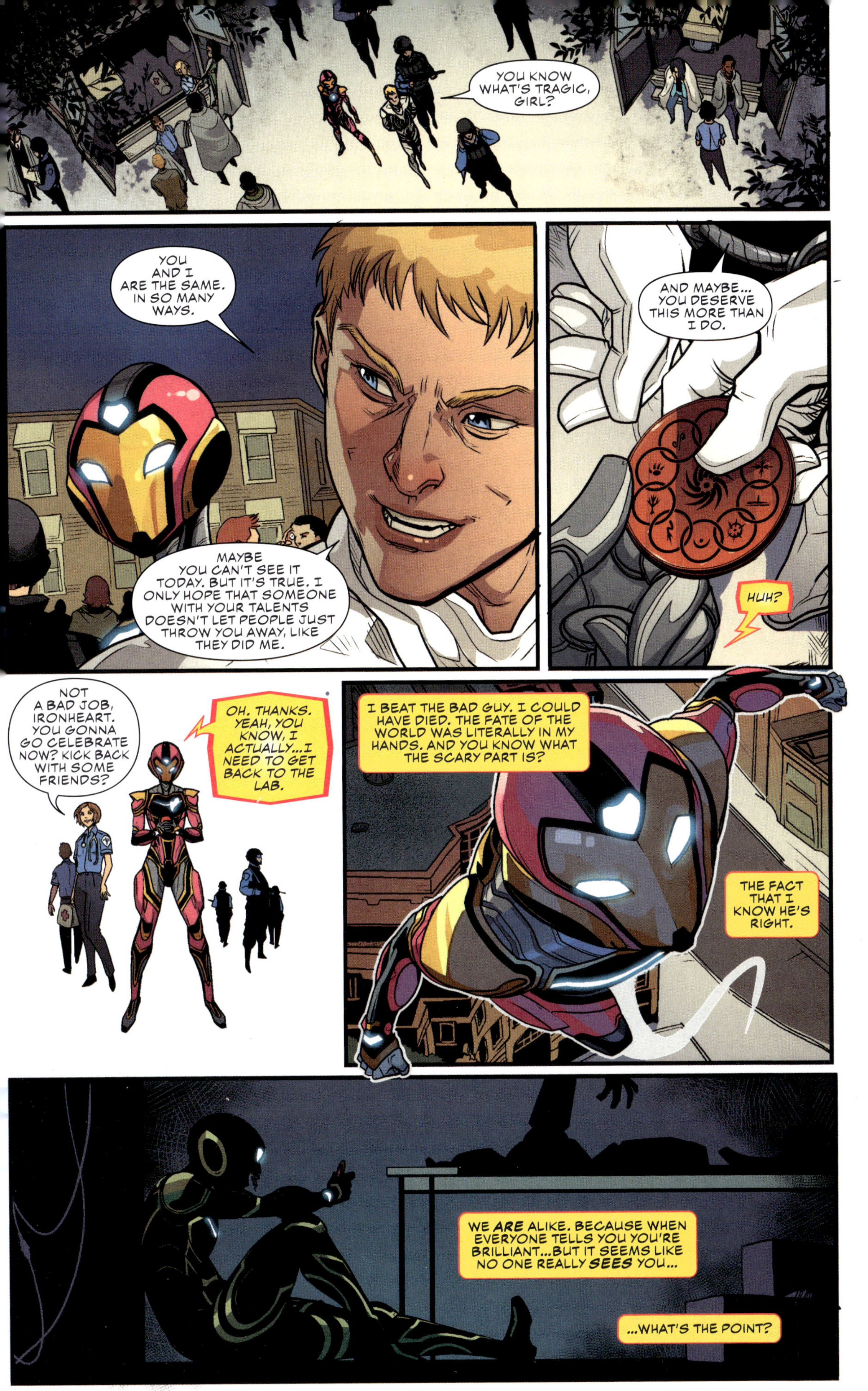
YOU KNOW WHAT'S TRAGIC, GIRL?
YOU AND I ARE THE SAME. IN SO MANY WAYS.
MAYBE YOU CAN'T SEE IT TODAY. BUT IT'S TRUE. I ONLY HOPE THAT SOMEONE WITH YOUR TALENTS DOESN'T LET PEOPLE JUST THROW YOU AWAY, LIKE THEY DID ME.
AND MAYBE... YOU DESERVE THIS MORE THAN I DO.
HUH?
NOT A BAD JOB, IRONHEART. YOU GONNA GO CELEBRATE NOW? KICK BACK WITH SOME FRIENDS?
OH. THANKS. YEAH, YOU KNOW, I ACTUALLY...I NEED TO GET BACK TO THE LAB.
I BEAT THE BAD GUY. I COULD HAVE DIED. THE FATE OF THE WORLD WAS LITERALLY IN MY HANDS. AND YOU KNOW WHAT THE SCARY PART IS?
THE FACT THAT I KNOW HE'S RIGHT.
WE ARE ALIKE. BECAUSE WHEN EVERYONE TELLS YOU YOU'RE BRILLIANT...BUT IT SEEMS LIKE NO ONE REALLY SEES YOU...
...WHAT'S THE POINT?

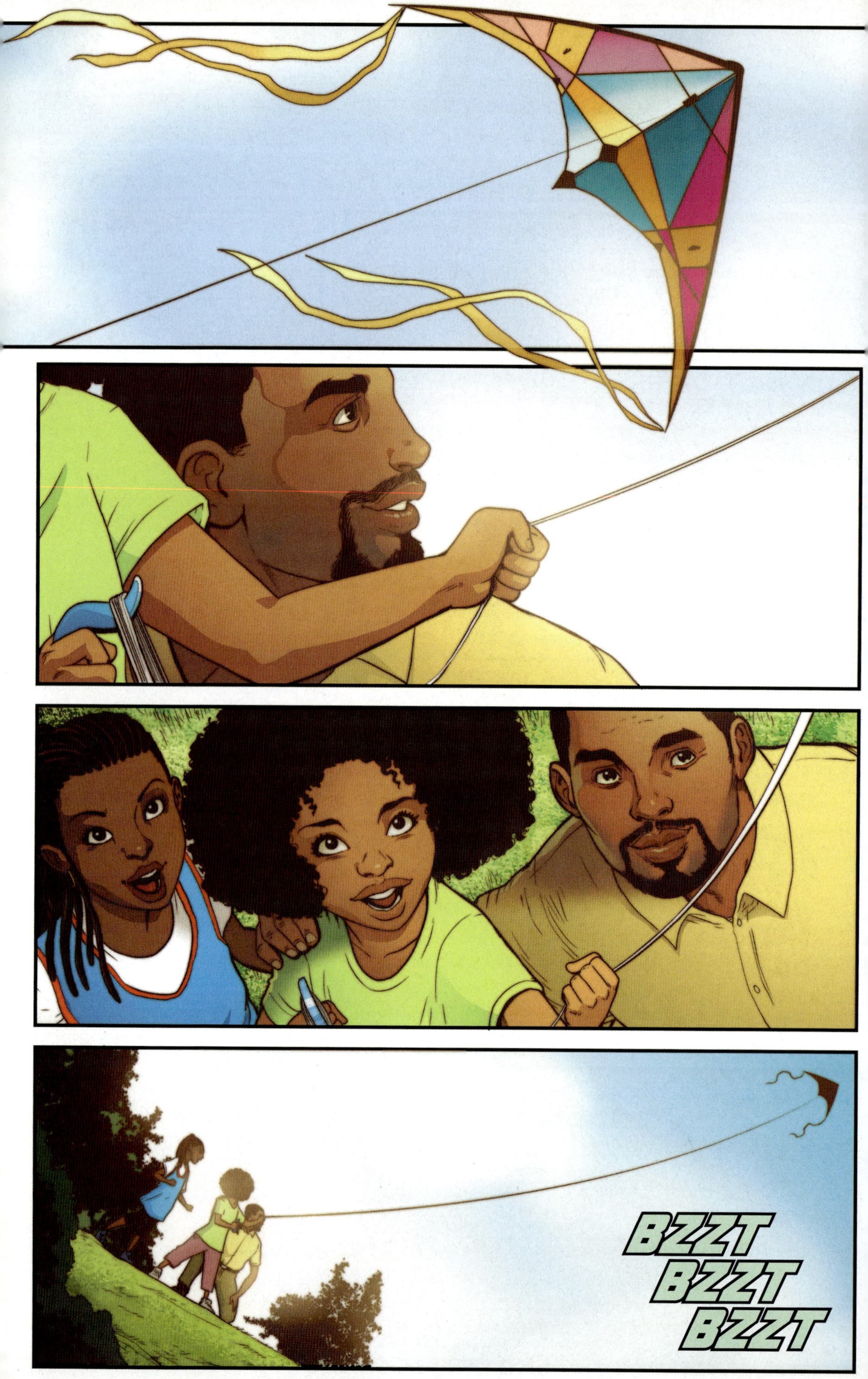
BZZT
BZZT
BZZT

BZZT
BZZT
BZZT
DADDY! NATALIE! I--WHA? MMPH.
UGH. WHO IS CALLING ME?
BZZT
BZZT
BZZT
WHERE... IS MY STUPID PHONE?
BZZT
BZZT
BZZT
MIT
BZZT
OH...OH WOW.

RIRI! HOW YOU BEEN?
HEL-- AHEM! HELLO! HI, XAVIER. WHY ARE YOU CALLING ME?
WELL, GOOD EVENING TO YOU TOO.
I'M, UH...I'M FREE TOMORROW, AND I WANTED TO SEE IF YOU WERE AROUND TO WATCH A MOVIE OR SOMETHING.
OH, WOW. WELL, I WOULD, BUT I'M ACTUALLY BACK AT M.I.T. THEY SET ME UP IN MY OWN LAB AND EVERYTHING! CHECK IT OUT.
SEE?

THAT'S... THAT'S AWESOME, RIRI.
BUT WHY ARE YOU THERE NOW? IT'S SUPER LATE AT NIGHT. AND I SAW YOU ON THE NEWS EARLIER. DIDN'T YOU HAVE KIND OF A LONG DAY?
I'M...RESEARCHING SOME STUFF. AND I'M TRYING TO GET THE A.I. GOING ON THIS NEW SUIT. IT'S NOT REALLY MY STRENGTH, BUT I'VE BEEN TEACHING MYSELF.
WHAT ARE YOU DOING UP?
JUST COULDN'T SLEEP.
I WAS SITTING HERE WATCHING ATTACK OF THE SPIDER PEOPLE FROM JUPITER AND I THOUGHT, WHY DON'T I GIVE MY FAMOUS NEIGHBOR A CALL?
HEY, HAVE YOU EVER--
XAVIER. HOW...HOW DID YOU GET MY NUMBER?

HUH? RIRI, I'VE KNOWN YOU SINCE WE WERE LITTLE KIDS.
YEAH, BUT I DON'T REMEMBER ACTUALLY GIVING YOU MY NUMBER. WHO GAVE YOU MY NUMBER?
OKAY, LOOK. MY MAMA TOLD ME TO CALL YOU. SHE WAS TALKING TO YOUR MAMA AND SHE WAS WORRIED ABOUT YOU. SHE SAID YOU DIDN'T HAVE ANY FRIENDS AT SCHOOL, AND--
OH, I GET IT. I'M A CHARITY CASE. REAL GOOD TO KNOW. HONESTLY, THOUGH?! NO NEED TO WASTE YOUR TIME ON ME, XAVIER. I'M GOOD.
HEY, CAN YOU CHILL FOR A SEC? IF YOU DON'T WANT TO TALK THAT'S FINE. I JUST THOUGHT--
I SAID I'M GOOD, OKAY? GOOD NIGHT!
KRAK
WAIT! HOLD UP!
WHAT DO YOU WANT?!
HOT

ARE THOSE...IS THAT...A GEORDI VISOR?
ARE YOU MAKING THAT FOR AN EXPERIMENT OR SOMETHING? IS IT GOING ON YOUR SUIT?
RIGHT THERE! ON YOUR TABLE.
COSPLAY.
HUH?
IT. IS. COSPLAY. IT'S **COSPLAY!** IT'S FOR A COSPLAY, OKAY? ANOTHER **LOSER** THING THAT I LIKE TO DO BECAUSE I'M A NERDY **LOSER** WITH **NO FRIENDS!**
WELL, I... I ACTUALLY...REALLY LIKE STAR TREK.
YOU DO?
SO UNDERRATED!
YEAH! I LIKE **THE NEXT GENERATION** BECAUSE OF GEORDI BUT HAVE YOU EVER WATCHED **DEEP SPACE NINE?**
YO, **HIGHLY** UNDERRATED. SISKO IS **THAT DUDE.**

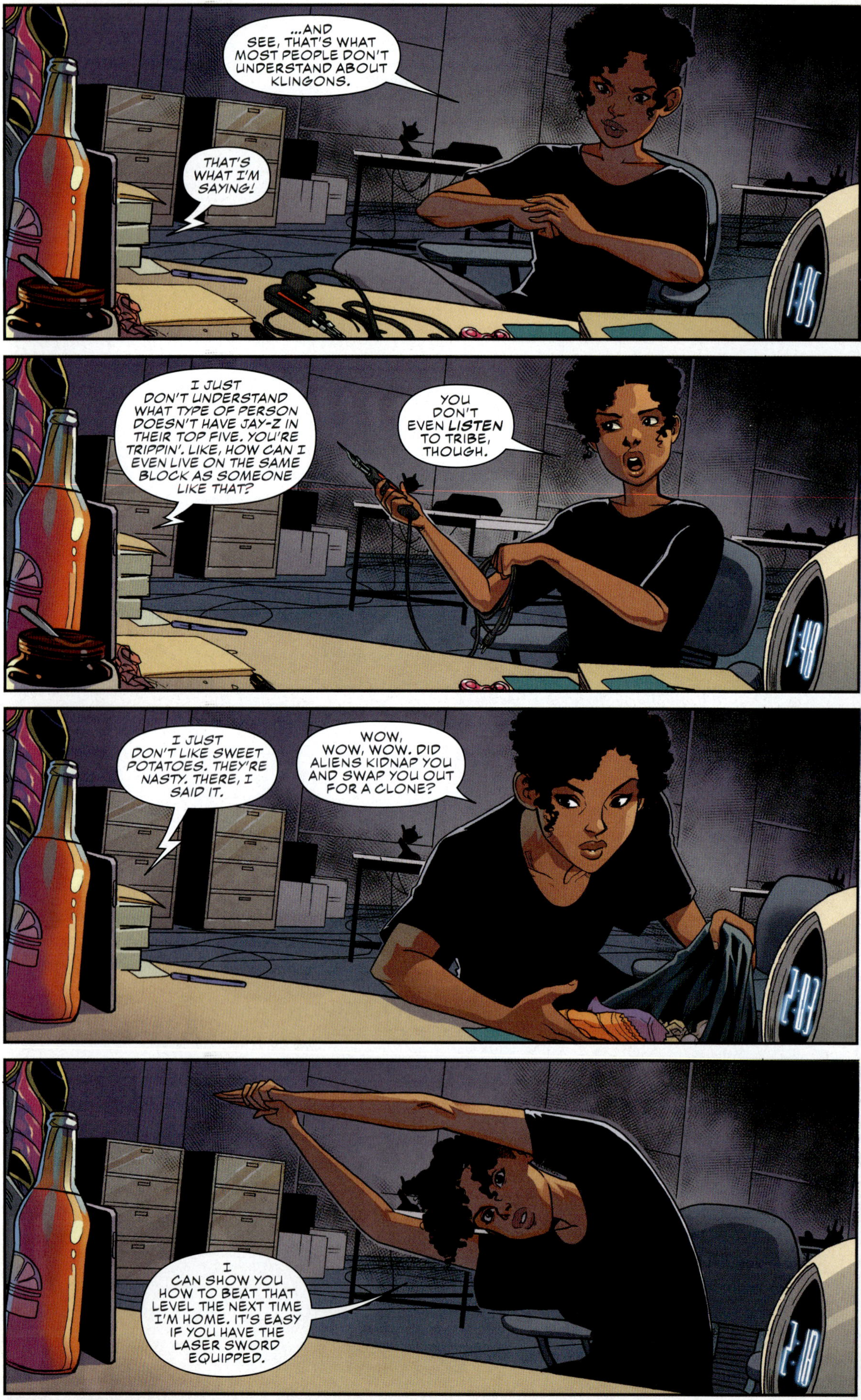
...AND SEE, THAT'S WHAT MOST PEOPLE DON'T UNDERSTAND ABOUT KLINGONS.
THAT'S WHAT I'M SAYING!
I JUST DON'T UNDERSTAND WHAT TYPE OF PERSON DOESN'T HAVE JAY-Z IN THEIR TOP FIVE. YOU'RE TRIPPIN'. LIKE, HOW CAN I EVEN LIVE ON THE SAME BLOCK AS SOMEONE LIKE THAT?
YOU DON'T EVEN LISTEN TO TRIBE, THOUGH.
1:05
1:48
I JUST DON'T LIKE SWEET POTATOES. THEY'RE NASTY. THERE, I SAID IT.
WOW, WOW, WOW. DID ALIENS KIDNAP YOU AND SWAP YOU OUT FOR A CLONE?
2:03
I CAN SHOW YOU HOW TO BEAT THAT LEVEL THE NEXT TIME I'M HOME. IT'S EASY IF YOU HAVE THE LASER SWORD EQUIPPED.
2:10

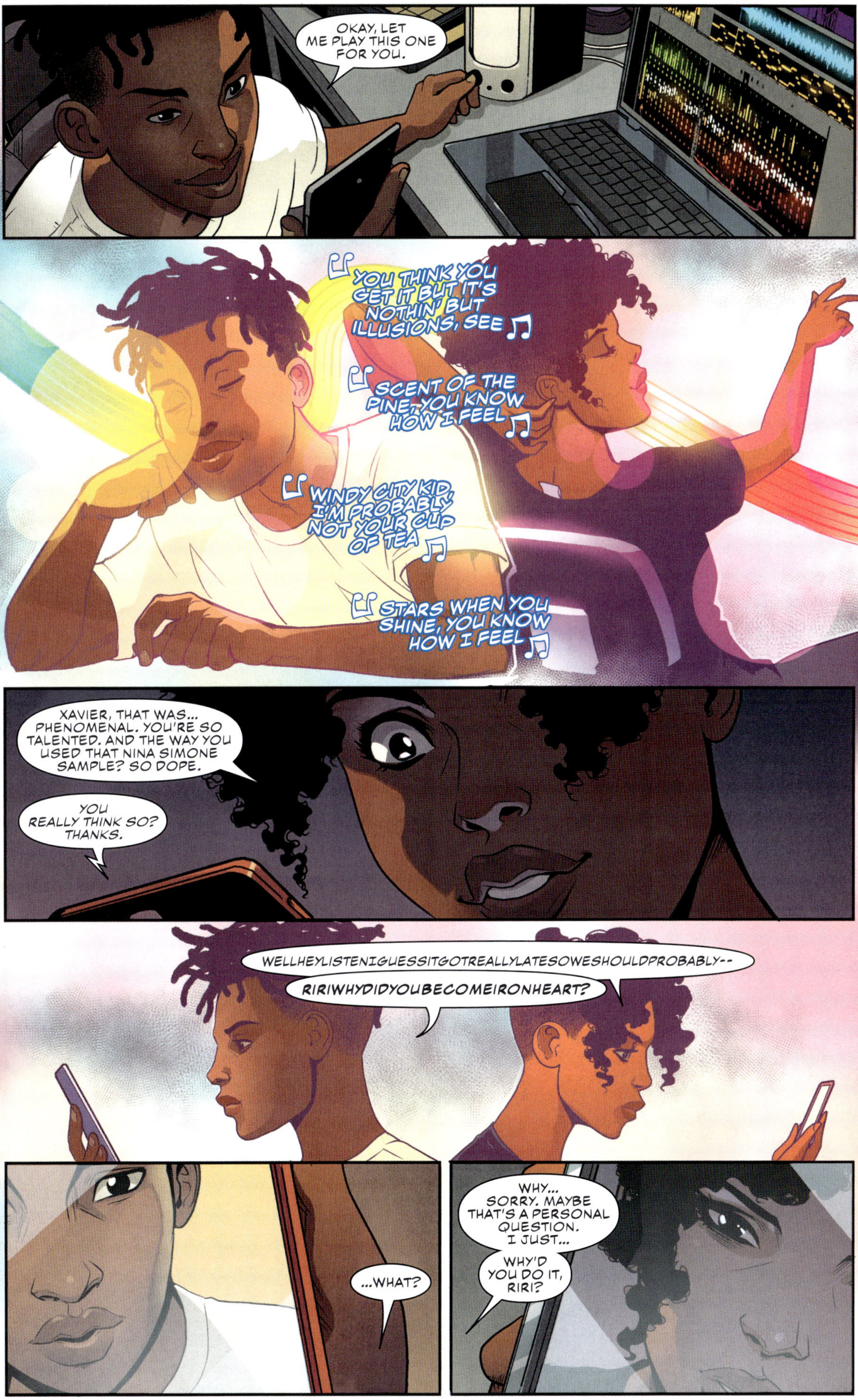
OKAY, LET ME PLAY THIS ONE FOR YOU.
YOU THINK YOU GET IT BUT IT'S NOTHIN' BUT ILLUSIONS, SEE ♫
SCENT OF THE PINE, YOU KNOW HOW I FEEL ♫
WINDY CITY KID, I'M PROBABLY NOT YOUR CUP OF TEA ♫
STARS WHEN YOU SHINE, YOU KNOW HOW I FEEL ♫
XAVIER, THAT WAS... PHENOMENAL. YOU'RE SO TALENTED. AND THE WAY YOU USED THAT NINA SIMONE SAMPLE? SO DOPE.
YOU REALLY THINK SO? THANKS.
WELLHEYLISTENIGUESSITGOTREALLYLATESOWESHOULDPROBABLY--
RIRIWHYDIDYOUBECOMEIRONHEART?
...WHAT?
WHY... SORRY. MAYBE THAT'S A PERSONAL QUESTION. I JUST...
WHY'D YOU DO IT, RIRI?

WELL, I WAS AT SCHOOL, AND I BUILT THE SUIT, AND...UM...
NO, I KNOW THAT'S HOW YOU DID IT. BUT...WHY DID YOU DO IT?
WHAT DO YOU MEAN, WHY? BECAUSE...I COULD? I DON'T KNOW.
OKAY, BUT, LIKE...YOU AND I BOTH KNOW WHAT IT'S LIKE WHERE YOU AND I COME FROM. NOTHING IS GUARANTEED. NOTHING IS PROMISED. WE'VE LOST SO MANY PEOPLE.
TRUST ME, I KNOW.
OH, RIRI...OH, GOSH. I'M SORRY. I DIDN'T--BUT THAT'S WHAT I MEAN!
WHAT IF SOMETHING HAPPENED TO YOU? YOU GO OUT THERE IN THAT SUIT AND YOU COULD GET HURT! WHY WOULD YOU DO THAT?
YOUR MOM, YOU KNOW, SHE PLAYS IT COOL BUT I KNOW SHE'S GOTTA BE WORRIED SICK, I GET WORRIED, WE ALL...
RIRI. YOU COULD DIE!

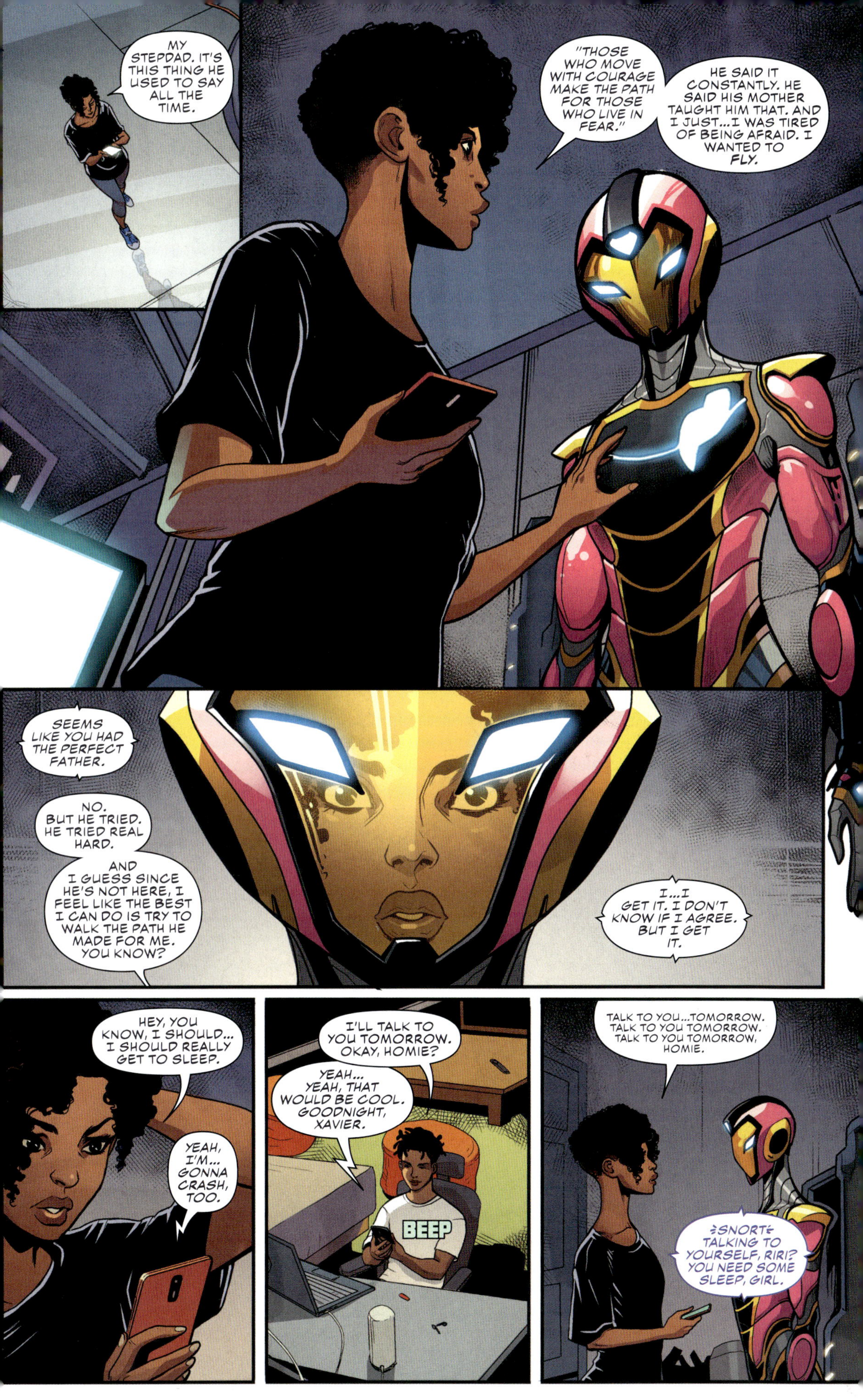

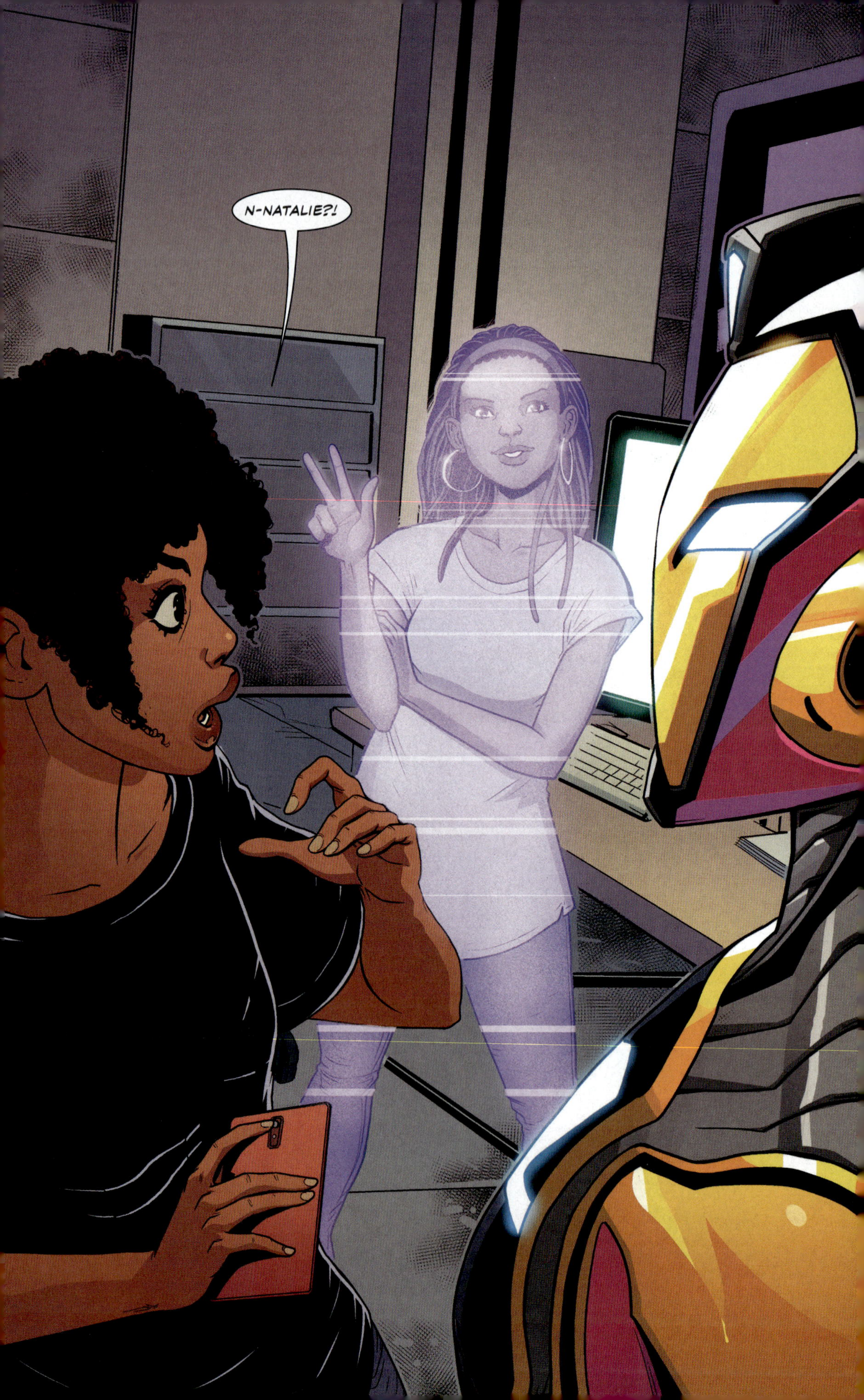
N-NATALIE?!

STEPHANIE HANS
#1 VARIANT

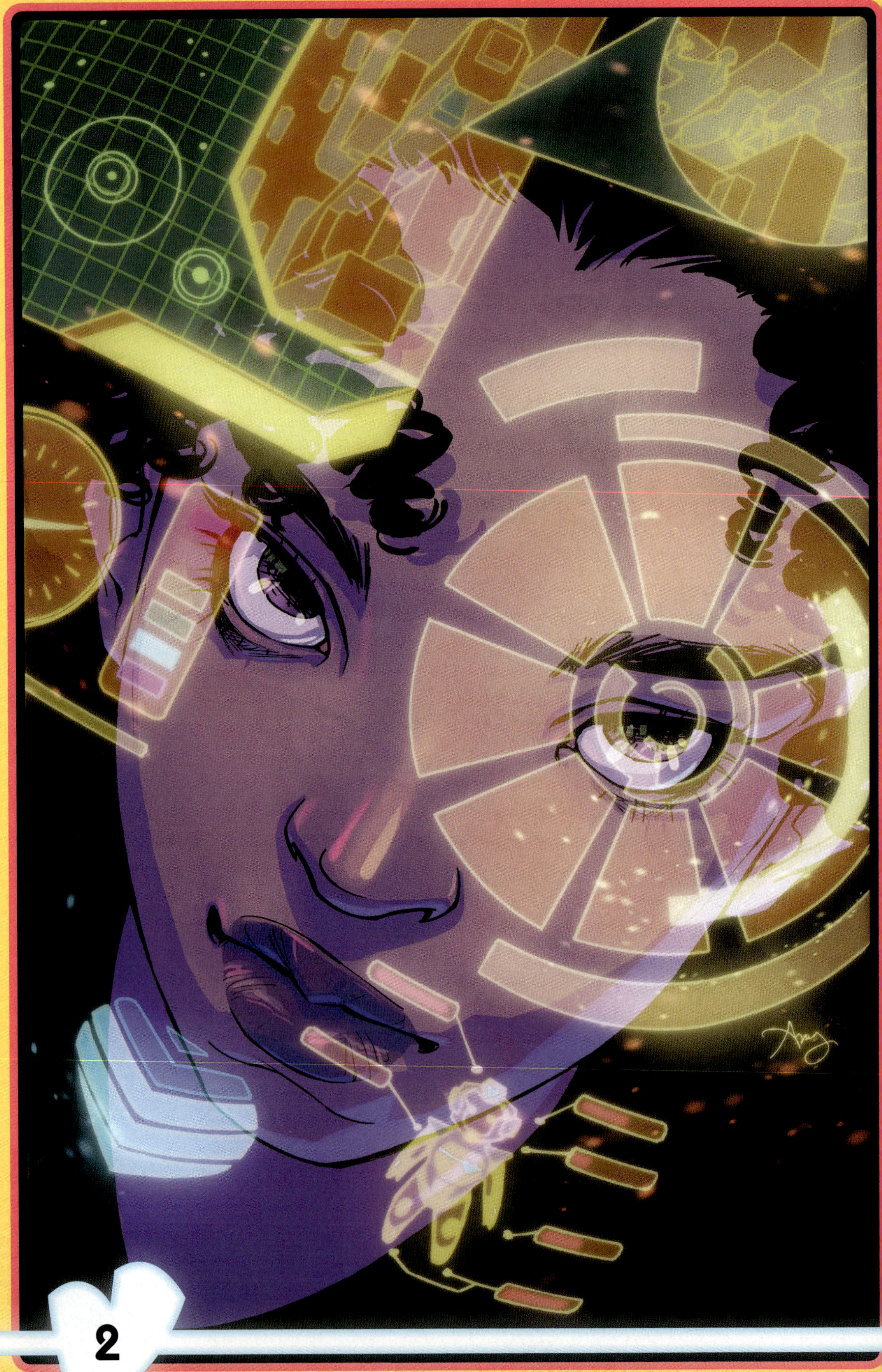

CHICAGO.
KING COLLEGE PREP HIGH SCHOOL. FIVE YEARS AGO.

ARGH! WHY WON'T THIS STUPID THING WORK?!

WOW, FOR REAL? IN FRONT OF THE KID?

HUSH! IF SHE WASN'T READY TO BE WITH THE GROWN-UPS, SHE WOULDN'T HAVE COME TO HIGH SCHOOL. RIGHT, SHORTY?

I... UM...

WE BETTER GET TO CLASS. YOU TOO, LI'L MAMA. YOU DON'T WANT DETENTION.

BUT MY...

...MY BOOKS ARE ALL IN HERE.

AY! WHAT YOU DOING? NO TEARS ALLOWED!

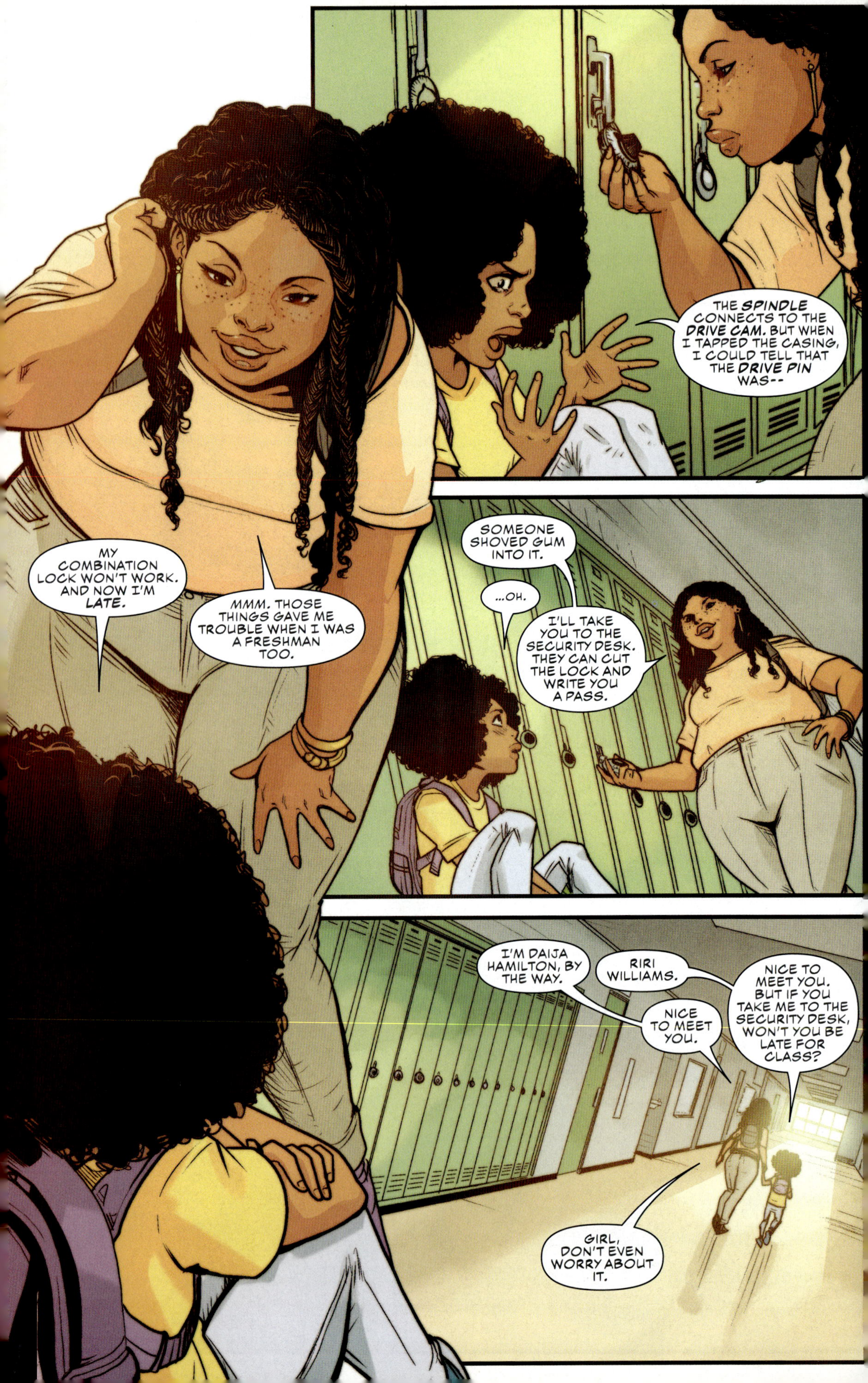
THE SPINDLE CONNECTS TO THE DRIVE CAM. BUT WHEN I TAPPED THE CASING, I COULD TELL THAT THE DRIVE PIN WAS--
MY COMBINATION LOCK WON'T WORK. AND NOW I'M LATE.
MMM. THOSE THINGS GAVE ME TROUBLE WHEN I WAS A FRESHMAN TOO.
SOMEONE SHOVED GUM INTO IT.
...OH.
I'LL TAKE YOU TO THE SECURITY DESK. THEY CAN CUT THE LOCK AND WRITE YOU A PASS.
I'M DAIJA HAMILTON, BY THE WAY.
RIRI WILLIAMS.
NICE TO MEET YOU.
NICE TO MEET YOU. BUT IF YOU TAKE ME TO THE SECURITY DESK, WON'T YOU BE LATE FOR CLASS?
GIRL, DON'T EVEN WORRY ABOUT IT.

"SOMETIMES YOU DO WHAT YOU GOTTA DO TO LOOK OUT FOR YOUR PEOPLE."

BOSTON.
DORCHESTER NEIGHBORHOOD. PRESENT DAY.

I SENT A PAYMENT LAST WEEK! I DON'T KNOW WHAT YOU WANT!

WE *OWN* YOU. IF WE WANT MORE MONEY, YOU GIVE IT.

HEY, WHAT ARE YOU DOING?

MIND YOUR OWN *BUSINESS*, OLD MAN!

THIS *IS* MY BUSINESS! WE'RE SICK OF YOU TERRORIZING THIS NEIGHBORHOOD!

MINH, PLEASE. THESE MEN ARE DANGEROUS!

WHAT ARE THEY GONNA DO, KILL ME? SO WHAT, I'M *OLD!*

OKAY. WE--

AUUGHH!

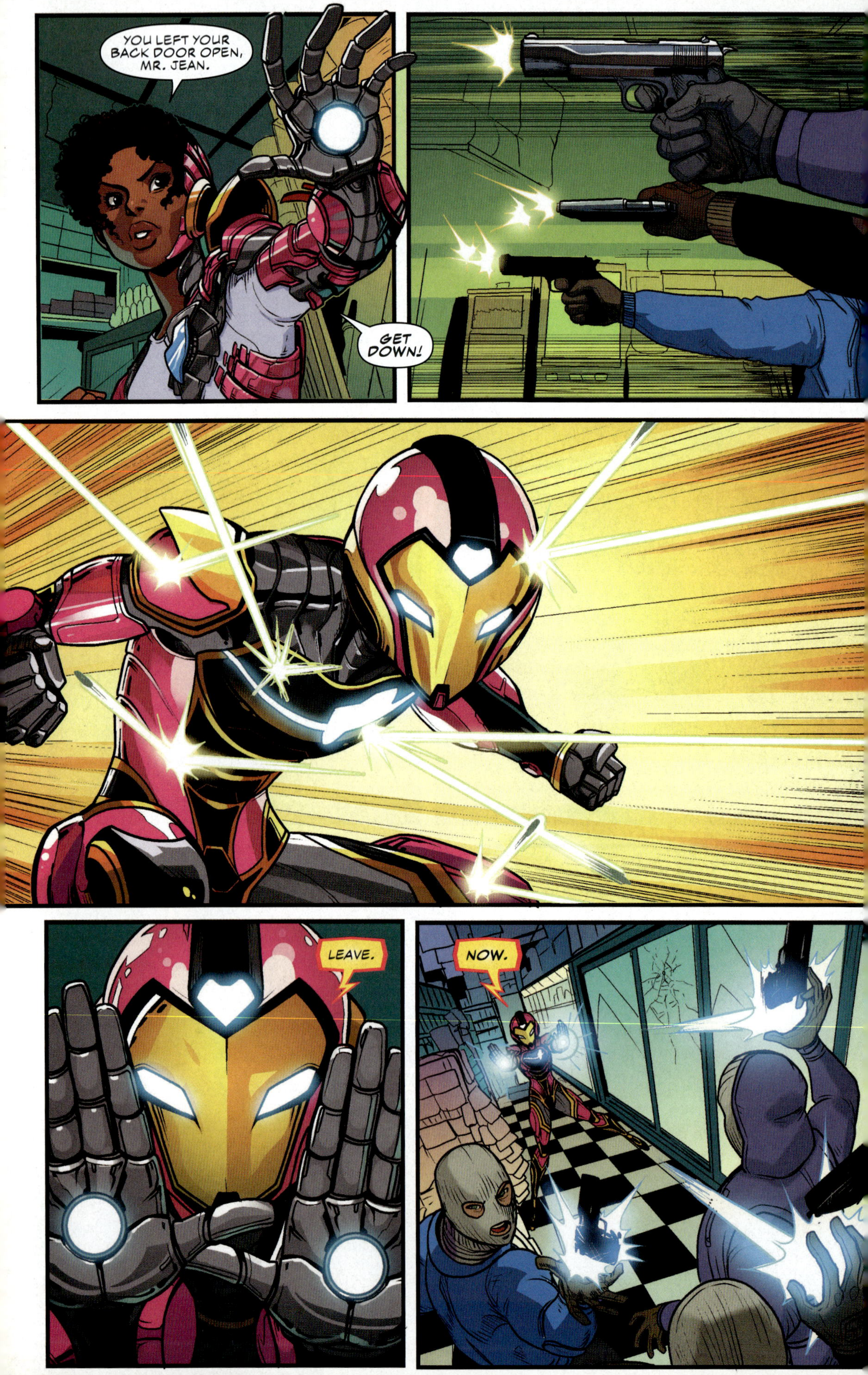
YOU LEFT YOUR BACK DOOR OPEN, MR. JEAN.
GET DOWN!
LEAVE.
NOW.

THANK YOU, LITTLE IRON.
IRONHEART.
YES, YES. THANK YOU.
ANY TIME. DO YOU MIND IF I PAY YOU FOR THESE LATER?
MR. JEAN, MAYBE I SHOULD GIVE YOU SOME KIND OF DISTRESS SIGNAL. I'VE BEEN WORKING ON A PROTOTYPE--
WHY? I WOULD BE HITTING THE BUTTON EVERY DAY. BETTER I GIVE THEM WHAT THEY WANT.
DON'T GIVE IN! IRONHEART CAN PROTECT US!
SHE CAN'T BE HERE ALL THE TIME!
I... I WISH I COULD BE. THERE ARE JUST SO MANY PEOPLE WHO NEED HELP.
YOU DO WHAT YOU CAN. AND IF THEY KILL ME, AT LEAST I LEAVE A HANDSOME CORPSE.
AAAAHAAAA! HA HA HA!
WE APPRECIATE YOU, GIRL.
BUT IT'S NOT FAIR. THE CITY SHOULD--
REEEE

YOU FORGOT WHO OWNS THIS NEIGHBORHOOD! THIS AIN'T A GAME!
SHE'S NOT SCARED OF YOU! YOU TRASH! WE'RE NOT AFRAID!
GET BACK INSIDE! EVERYBODY GET BACK!
GET BACK! GET BEHIND ME! GET BACK. GET... GET...
GIRLS, GET BACK!
--UNDER ATTACK, RIRI! SNAP OUT OF IT! YOU'RE SUSTAINING HEAVY FIRE! COME BACK, GIRL!

N-NATALIE?
GET IT TOGETHER, RIRI! GET YOUR HEAD IN THE GAME, 'CAUSE WE AIN'T GOING OUT LIKE THIS!
AAAAARGH!
GAAAAAHHHHHHH!
IS EVERYONE OKAY? NO ONE'S HURT?
EXCEPT YOU, CHOU!
YOU WERE OUT OF IT! THEY WERE JUST SHOOTING AND SHOOTING AND YOU WEREN'T--
YEAH. SORRY. BUT EVERYONE IS OKAY NOW.
BUT WHAT--
I HAVE TO GO, OKAY? I'LL-- I'LL SEE Y'ALL LATER.
WAIT!

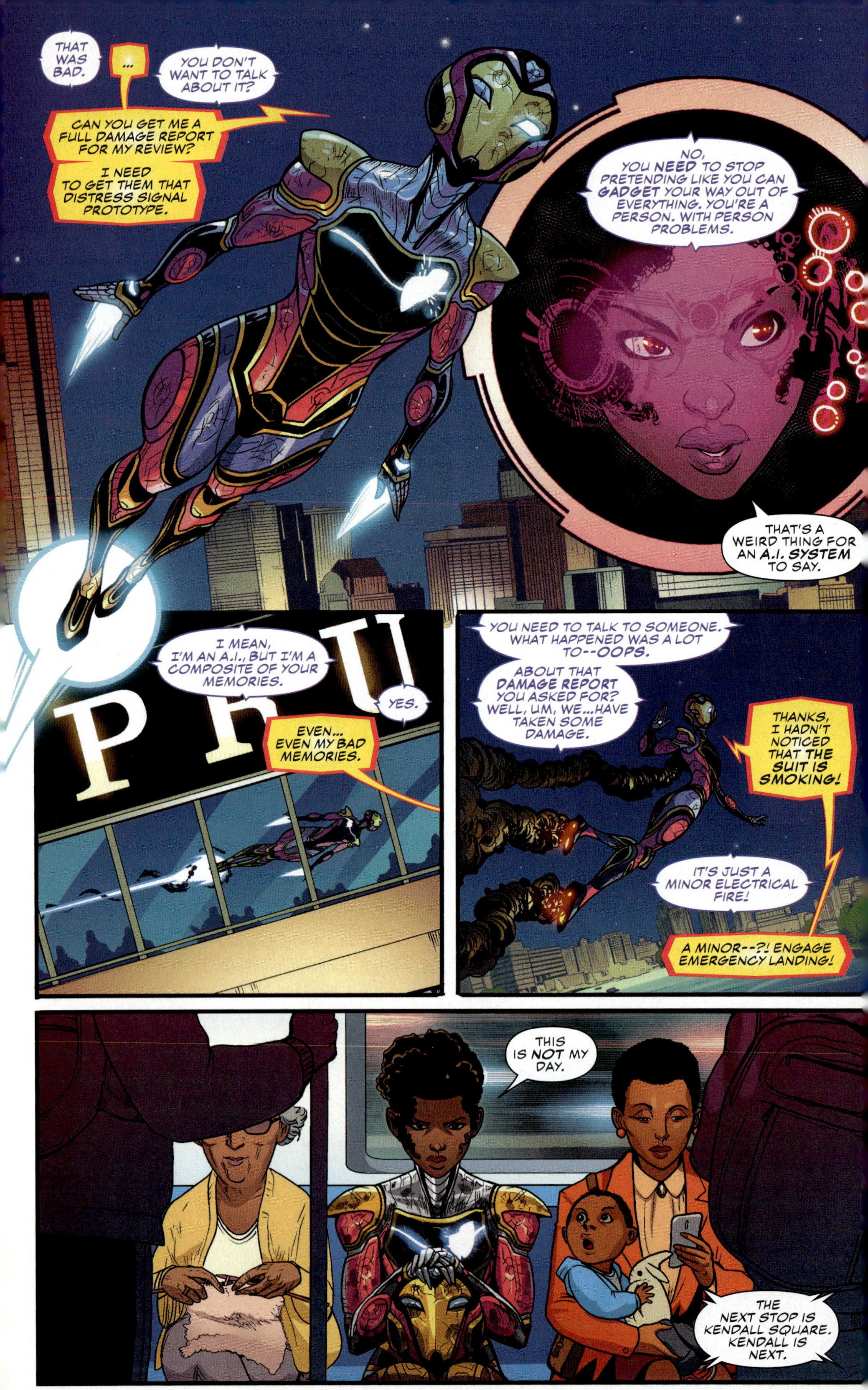

THAT WAS BAD.
...
YOU DON'T WANT TO TALK ABOUT IT?
CAN YOU GET ME A FULL DAMAGE REPORT FOR MY REVIEW?
I NEED TO GET THEM THAT DISTRESS SIGNAL PROTOTYPE.
NO, YOU **NEED** TO STOP PRETENDING LIKE YOU CAN **GADGET** YOUR WAY OUT OF EVERYTHING. YOU'RE A PERSON. WITH PERSON PROBLEMS.
THAT'S A WEIRD THING FOR AN ***A.I. SYSTEM*** TO SAY.
I MEAN, I'M AN A.I., BUT I'M A COMPOSITE OF YOUR MEMORIES.
PRU
YES.
EVEN... EVEN MY BAD MEMORIES.
YOU NEED TO TALK TO SOMEONE. WHAT HAPPENED WAS A LOT TO--**OOPS.**
ABOUT THAT **DAMAGE REPORT** YOU ASKED FOR? WELL, UM, WE...HAVE TAKEN SOME DAMAGE.
THANKS, I HADN'T NOTICED THAT **THE SUIT IS SMOKING!**
IT'S JUST A MINOR ELECTRICAL FIRE!
A MINOR--?! ENGAGE EMERGENCY LANDING!
THIS IS **NOT** MY DAY.
THE NEXT STOP IS KENDALL SQUARE. KENDALL IS NEXT.

MY GAUNTLET RETRACTION ISN'T WORKING. I'M GOING TO NEED TO DO A MANUAL REMOVAL AND--
M.I.T.
COME ON, NOT THIS AGAIN.
DEAN BRYANT, I THOUGHT WE HAD A DISCUSSION ABOUT UNAUTHORIZED VISITORS IN MY LAB.
HELLO, MS. WILLIAMS! THESE ARE AUTHORIZED VISITORS FROM ALCHEMAX, INTERESTED IN SPONSORSHIP OPPORTUNITIES.
WHAT IS THIS, ANOTHER GIRL GENIUS?
WHAT DO YOU CALL IT?
THE NEURO-AUTONOMOUS TECHNICAL ASSISTANT & LABORATORY INTELLIGENCE ENTITY.
NATALIE. SHE'S A SHE, NOT AN IT. AND SHE'S PROPRIETARY TECHNOLOGY. NO PHOTOS.
YOU SEEM TO LACK CLARITY. YOU ARE THE ONLY UNDERGRADUATE WITH A LAB--
LAST I CHECKED THERE'S NOT EXACTLY A SUPER HERO STUDENT UNION.
THERE. ARE. COSTS. AS LONG AS YOU WORK UNDER THIS INSTITUTION, YOU PLAY BY OUR RULES.
...OKAY. MESSAGE RECEIVED.
GENTLEMEN, LET'S GO.
GAAAAAHHHHH! WHY DOES HE THINK HE CAN JUST PARADE PEOPLE IN AND OUT OF HERE?
BECAUSE HE CAN.
BUT IF IT MAKES YOU FEEL ANY BETTER, THEY WERE ALL ON OUR WI-FI, SO I HACKED THEIR PHONES AND DELETED ALL THE PICTURES.
YOU KNOW...THAT DOES MAKE ME FEEL BETTER.

THIS ISN'T AS BAD AS IT LOOKED INITIALLY. I FIXED THE SHORT THAT CAUSED THE FIRE. THE REST OF THE PROBLEMS ARE COSMETIC.
RIRI-- TAKE A LOOK AT THIS.
KEYWORD ALERT:
CHICAGO
LOCAL WOMAN STILL MISSING
THIS MISSING GIRL, ISN'T SHE...
OH MY GOSH.
AND NOW SHE'S MISSING CLASS AND SO AM I. IF WE'RE GONNA HAVE A LITTLE KID IN THIS SCHOOL SOMEBODY BETTER LOOK OUT FOR HER.
LET'S GO HOME.

SOUTH SHORE, CHICAGO.
WE'RE DOOMED! IT'S ALL OVER NOW!
DON'T GIVE UP HOPE! THE IRON WARRIOR HAS COME TO SAVE THE CITY!

THIS MOVIE NEVER GETS OLD.
WATCH THIS PART, RIRI. THE IRON WARRIOR IS GONNA CUT DUDE'S HEAD OFF. BLAOW.
UH-HUH.

YOU LOOKING INTO THE WHOLE DAIJA THING, HUH?
INDEXING ALL THE NEWS COVERAGE OF HER DISAPPEARANCE.
AND?
HONESTLY, THERE'S...SO LITTLE, XAVIER. HARDLY ANY DETAILS. LIKE NO ONE IS REALLY LOOKING FOR HER.
I MET HER ONCE AT MY COUSIN'S BIRTHDAY. SHE SEEMED NICE. GOOD WITH KIDS.
YOU TWO WANT SOME POP?
YES, PLEASE!
WERE YOU ALL TALKING ABOUT DAIJA?
YES. LOOKS LIKE I'M GONNA HAVE TO INVESTIGATE ON MY OWN.
I JUST SAW HER MOTHER AT THE GROCERY STORE A COUPLE WEEKS AGO. SHE TOLD ME DAIJA WAS DOING GOOD.
SHE WAS IN NIGHT CLASSES PART TIME AND HAD AN INTERNSHIP WITH SOMEBODY ON CITY COUNCIL.
IT'S SO SAD.
NOTHING BUT BAD NEWS...
--WAVE OF ROBBERIES.
POLICE ARE ADVISING RESIDENTS THAT TEENS AND EVEN CHILDREN HAVE BEEN REPORTED STEALING ELECTRONICS--

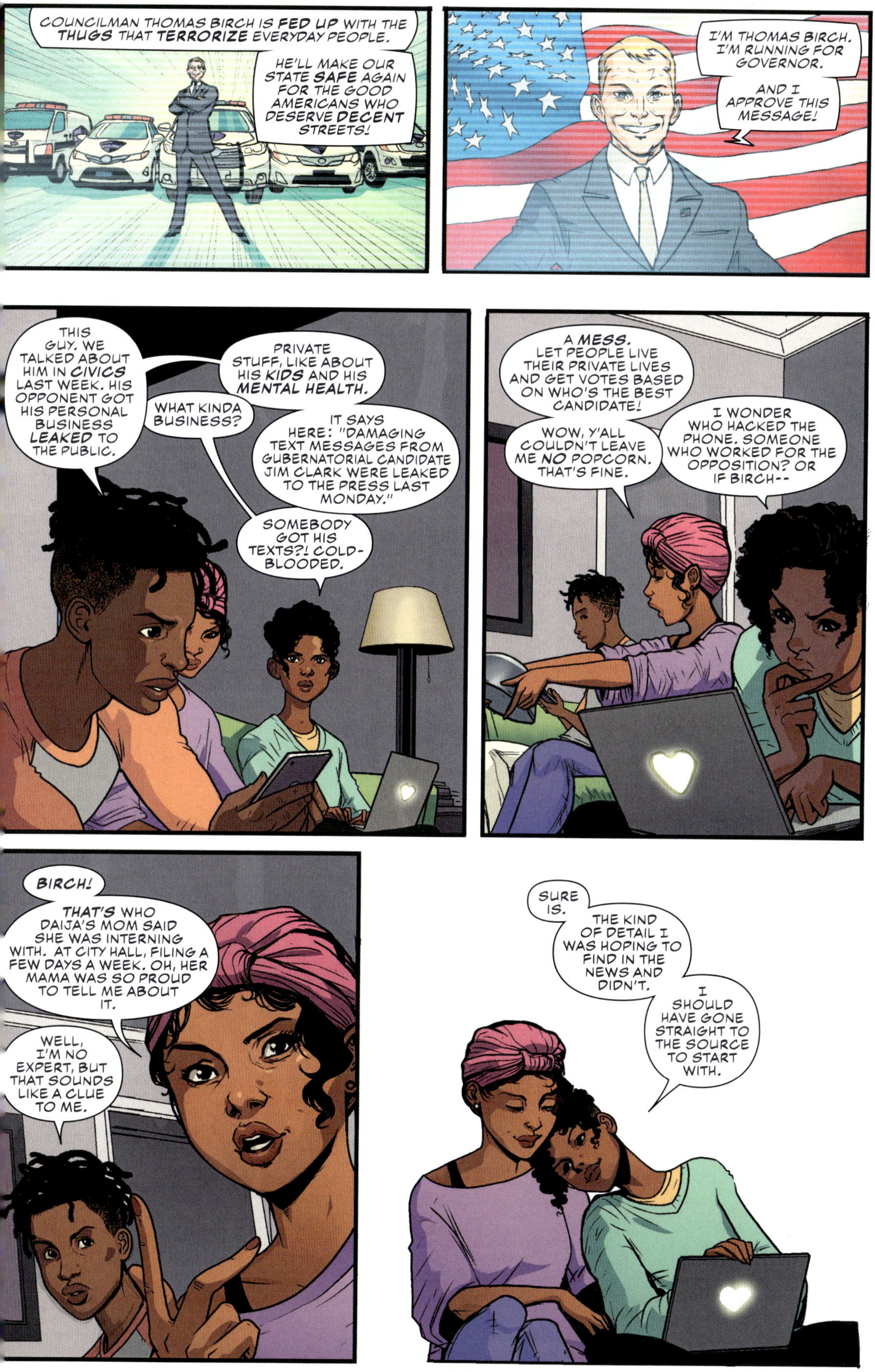
COUNCILMAN THOMAS BIRCH IS FED UP WITH THE THUGS THAT TERRORIZE EVERYDAY PEOPLE.
HE'LL MAKE OUR STATE SAFE AGAIN FOR THE GOOD AMERICANS WHO DESERVE DECENT STREETS!
I'M THOMAS BIRCH. I'M RUNNING FOR GOVERNOR.
AND I APPROVE THIS MESSAGE!
THIS GUY. WE TALKED ABOUT HIM IN CIVICS LAST WEEK. HIS OPPONENT GOT HIS PERSONAL BUSINESS LEAKED TO THE PUBLIC.
WHAT KINDA BUSINESS?
PRIVATE STUFF, LIKE ABOUT HIS KIDS AND HIS MENTAL HEALTH.
IT SAYS HERE: "DAMAGING TEXT MESSAGES FROM GUBERNATORIAL CANDIDATE JIM CLARK WERE LEAKED TO THE PRESS LAST MONDAY."
SOMEBODY GOT HIS TEXTS?! COLD-BLOODED.
A MESS. LET PEOPLE LIVE THEIR PRIVATE LIVES AND GET VOTES BASED ON WHO'S THE BEST CANDIDATE!
WOW, Y'ALL COULDN'T LEAVE ME NO POPCORN. THAT'S FINE.
I WONDER WHO HACKED THE PHONE. SOMEONE WHO WORKED FOR THE OPPOSITION? OR IF BIRCH--
BIRCH!
THAT'S WHO DAIJA'S MOM SAID SHE WAS INTERNING WITH. AT CITY HALL, FILING A FEW DAYS A WEEK. OH, HER MAMA WAS SO PROUD TO TELL ME ABOUT IT.
WELL, I'M NO EXPERT, BUT THAT SOUNDS LIKE A CLUE TO ME.
SURE IS.
THE KIND OF DETAIL I WAS HOPING TO FIND IN THE NEWS AND DIDN'T.
I SHOULD HAVE GONE STRAIGHT TO THE SOURCE TO START WITH.

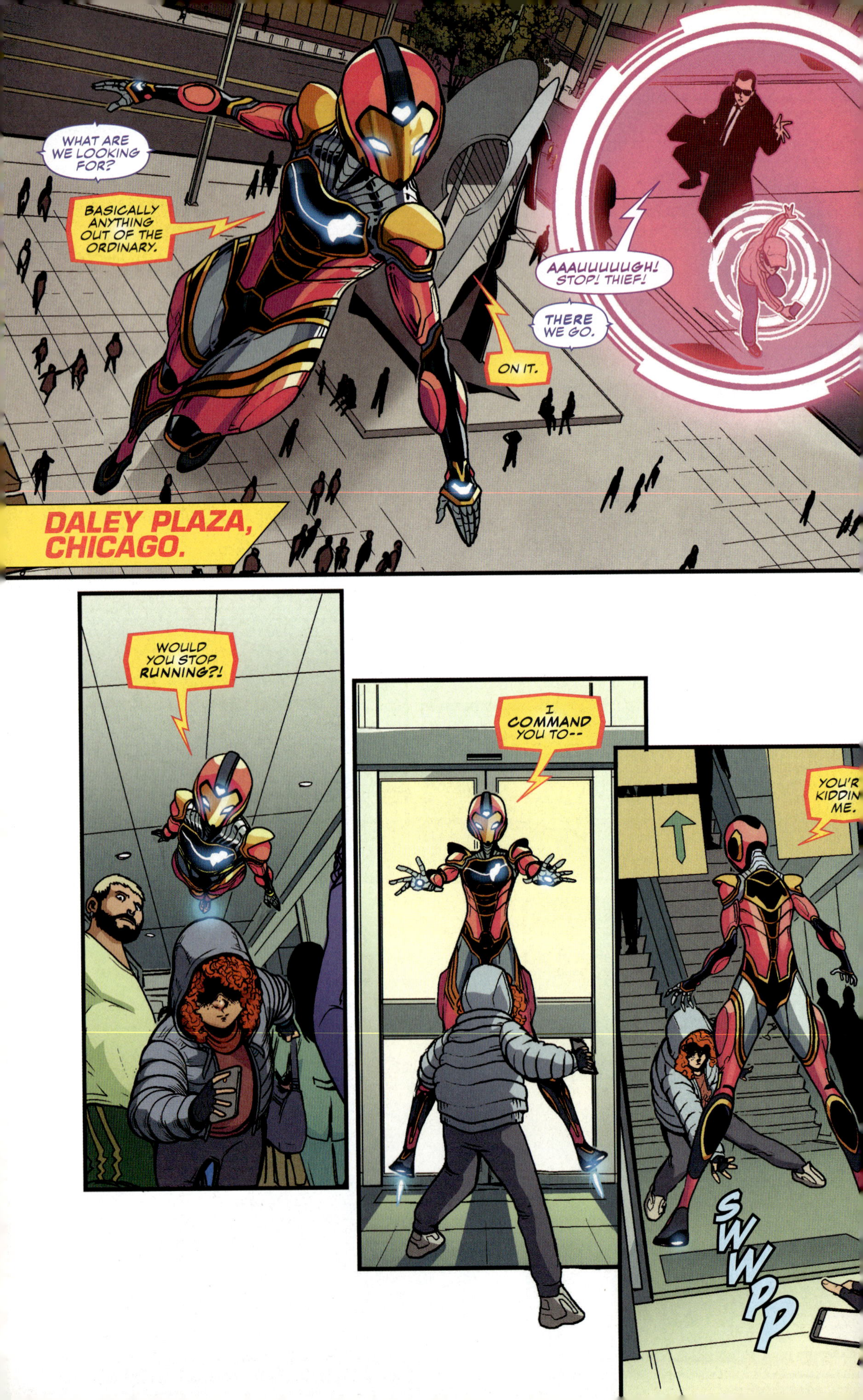

WHAT ARE WE LOOKING FOR?
BASICALLY ANYTHING OUT OF THE ORDINARY.
AAAUUUUUGH! STOP! THIEF!
THERE WE GO.
ON IT.
DALEY PLAZA, CHICAGO.
WOULD YOU STOP RUNNING?!
I COMMAND YOU TO--
YOU'R KIDDIN ME.
SWPP

GOTCHA NOW--
HEY, WHAT?
CATCH!
SHE'S FAST.
WELL, I'M FASTER.
LOST HER.
LUCKILY, YOU HAVE ME. AND I HAVE VISUAL CONFIRMATION.
MEANING I CAN SEE BUDDY RUNNING OVER THAT WAY, TOWARD THE METRA TRACKS.
ROGER ROGER.

THAT'S ENOUGH. THERE'S NO ONE HERE FOR ANY MORE HANDOFFS, SO YOU'LL HAVE TO--
OH MY GOSH.
YOU'RE JUST A... WHAT ARE YOU, 9?
I'M-- *HICCUP* I'M 10.
I DIDN'T WANNA DO THIS! THEY TOLD ME I HAD TO OR ELSE!
HEY. TAKE A BREATH. I'M NOT GONNA HURT YOU.
WHO TOLD YOU TO DO THIS?
THEY'RE GONNA BE SO MAD! I'M IN HUGE TROUBLE. HERE! I'M SORRY!
WAIT A SEC!
YOU GONNA GO AFTER HIM?
I DUNNO. MAYBE WE--
WHOA, RIRI! INCOMING!

WHERE DID THESE GUYS EVEN COME FROM?!
NO IDEA!
WHY WON'T YOU STAND STILL?!
OOF!
IF YOU THINK YOU'RE GOING TO INTERFERE WITH OUR BUSINESS, YOU'RE A FOOL.
AAHHHHHH!
UNKNOWN
ATTRIBUTES:
EXPERT HAND-TO-HAND
COMBAT.
SUPER SPEED.
THEY'RE TOO FAST! AND IT'S LIKE THEY KNOW ALL THE WEAKEST POINTS OF MY ARMOR!
DON'T PANIC. IF THEY KNOW ALL ITS WEAKNESSES, FORGET THE ARMOR FOR A SECOND.
JUST BE RIRI. WHAT WOULD RIRI DO?

THAT'S RIGHT, GIVE IN. THE WELLSPRING OF POWER, BEYOND YOUR COMPREHENSION, FLOWS THROUGH US.
YOU CAN'T POSSIBLY--
URRK!
AAAUUUGHH!
I HOPE YOU ENJOYED GETTING THE DROP ON ME.
BECAUSE IT'S NEVER HAPPENING AGAIN.
ESPECIALLY ONCE I KNOW WHO YOU ARE.
YOU CAN NEVER KNOW US.
THE CIRCLE SURROUNDS US. THE CIRCLE EXCEEDS US.
AAAAAH!
DID THEY-- DID THAT JUST--
NO. THEY'RE NOT DEAD. JUST DISAPPEARED.
BUT HOW?

SO YOU'RE NOT EVEN GONNA DO ANYTHING?!
HERE YOU GO.
OH MY GOSH! THANKS, IRON CHICK!
CHICAGO POLICE
IT'S IRONHEART. SEE, THERE'S A HEART ON MY HELMET. HEART. IRONHEART.
I TELL YA, THE CITY IS GETTING MORE DANGEROUS THAN EVER. HE STOLE MY PHONE!
IN BROAD DAYLIGHT?! DOWNTOWN!
POLICE EVERYWHERE! THEY DON'T EVEN CARE!
HEY! BE ALERT!
YOU'RE WELCOME!
SO I GUESS WE NEED TO RESEARCH THE THING OF THE THING.
WELLSPRING OF POWER.
LIKE I SAID.
MISSING
THAT WAS EMBARRASSING. I ALMOST GOT GOT.
BUT THEY DEFINITELY WERE MAKING THOSE KIDS STEAL PHONES.
I WONDER IF THEY'RE ALSO...

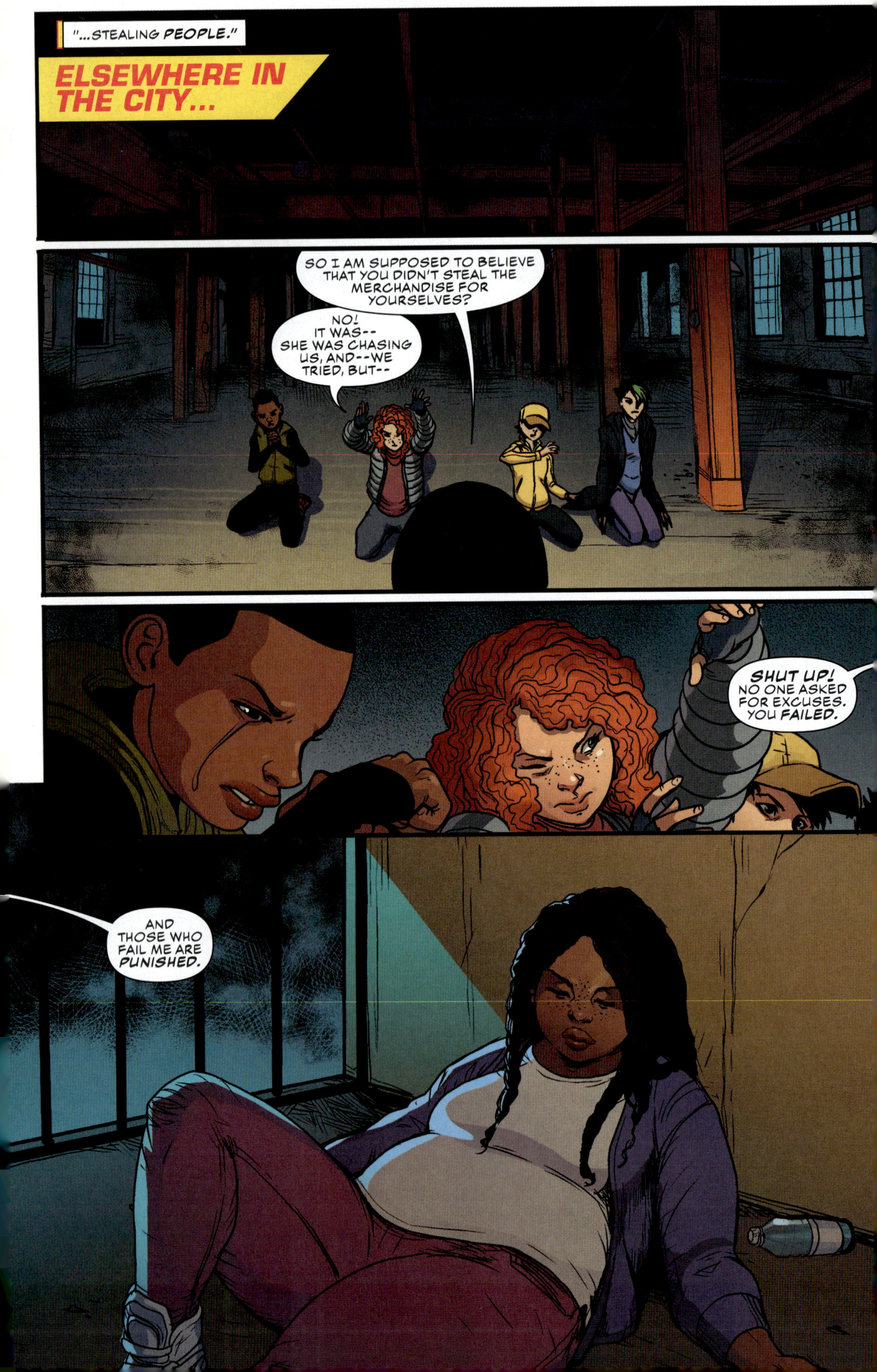

"...STEALING PEOPLE."
ELSEWHERE IN THE CITY...
SO I AM SUPPOSED TO BELIEVE THAT YOU DIDN'T STEAL THE MERCHANDISE FOR YOURSELVES?
NO! IT WAS-- SHE WAS CHASING US, AND--WE TRIED, BUT--
SHUT UP! NO ONE ASKED FOR EXCUSES. YOU FAILED.
AND THOSE WHO FAIL ME ARE PUNISHED.

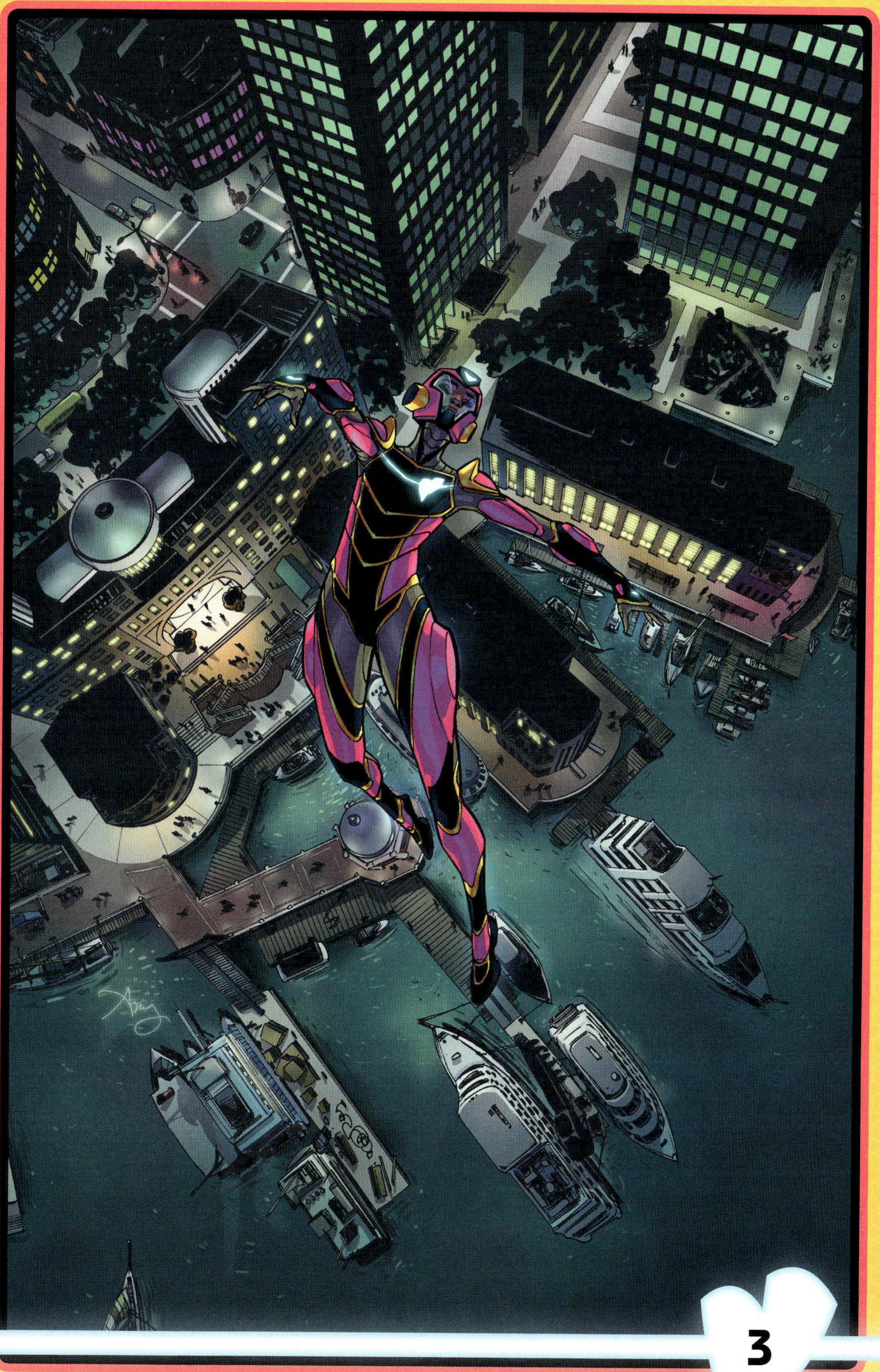

TWO YEARS AGO.
MARTIN LUTHER
HIGH SCHOOL
STATES OF MATTER.
ONE OF THE FIRST CONCEPTS IN PHYSICS I REMEMBER LEARNING. I WAS PROBABLY THREE YEARS OLD.
MOST PEOPLE DON'T KNOW GLASS IS ACTUALLY A LIQUID.
HERE, HOLD THIS UP!
ITS ATOMS JUST MOVE SO SLOWLY THAT WE CAN'T TELL.
CHK
SOMETHING THAT APPEARS UNCHANGING CAN BE SHIFTING CONSTANTLY BEFORE OUR EYES.
FLOWING.
JUST A SECOND, RIRI. I'M GOING TO GET YOU SOME FLOWERS TO HOLD. WON'T THAT BE NICE? IT'LL LOOK NICE.
AND WE DON'T EVEN NOTICE.

OH MOMMY, THAT'S--
I'M DAIJA. WE WENT TO SCHOOL TOGETHER.
SO NICE TO MEET YOU!
RIRI NEVER TOLD ME SHE HAD A FRIEND! WHAT YEAR DID YOU GRADUATE?
ACTUALLY, I DIDN'T. I HAD SOME FAMILY CIRCUMSTANCES, AND...I BEEN HELPING MY MOM OUT...
GOOD FOR YOU, SWEETHEART. SOMETIMES THE ROAD GETS A LITTLE SHAKY, BUT THAT'S GOOD THAT YOU CAN HELP YOUR FAMILY.
COME BY THE HOUSE! WE HAVE A CARAMEL CAKE AND I MIGHT EAT THE WHOLE DOGGONE THING MYSELF. RIGHT, RIRI?
HM? OH. DEFINITELY.
I'D... I'D LIKE THAT.

NOW.
AY, RIRI, WHAT YOU ON TODAY? YOU WANNA PLAY SOME--
OHHHH, THIS LOOKS LIKE A VERY SERIOUS SUPER HERO THING.
HEY, XAVIER.
IT'S A MAP OF ALL THE RECENT THEFTS.
THEY'RE USING KIDS TO STEAL-- I FEEL LIKE WHOEVER'S BEHIND IT MIGHT HAVE DAIJA. TRYING TO TRIANGULATE SOME LIKELY LOCATIONS FOR HER.
THIS DON'T LOOK LIKE SOMETHING YOU GET DOWN THE BLOCK AT BIG TOMMY'S USED ELECTRONICS EMPORIUM.
IT'S...ON LOAN. FROM M.I.T. IT'S NOT AS COMPLICATED AS IT LOOKS--JUST AN LCD PROJECTOR THAT I RIGGED TO INTERFACE WITH POLICE REPORTS CROSS-REFERENCED WITH ARCGIS.
CAN I HELP? I'LL BE THE GUY WHO TAPES THE PICTURES OF SUSPECTS TO THE WALL AND TIES A BUNCH OF STRINGS BETWEEN THEM.
THAT ONLY WORKS WHEN YOU HAVE A LIST OF SUSPECTS. WE AIN'T GOT THAT.
NO. BUT WE DO HAVE...
...A LIST OF VICTIMS. MAYBE THE PATTERN ISN'T WHERE, IT'S WHO.
REPORT FILED BY:
RICE, MALCOLM
WHY DIDN'T I THINK OF THAT?
YOU DON'T WATCH ENOUGH TV.

RIRI WILLIAMS. JUST WHAT ARE YOU DOING?
OH! HI, MOM. I'M...UM... WORKING?
WORKING. SHE SAYS SHE'S WORKING.
OOP.
YOU KNOW WHERE YOU'RE SUPPOSED TO BE WORKING? AT SCHOOL!
HOW ARE YOU EVEN PASSING YOUR CLASSES?
N.A.T.A.L.I.E. IS GOING TO LECTURES FOR ME.
SPEAK UP!
N.A.T.A.L.I.E. IS GOING TO LECTURES FOR ME!
M.I.T.
AREN'T YOU, UH, GONNA TAKE NOTES...?
I AM TAKING NOTES. AREN'T YOU GONNA MIND YOUR BUSINESS?
YOU DIDN'T EARN THE PRIVILEGE OF GOING TO M.I.T. JUST SO YOUR NARROW BEHIND CAN SIT AT HOME. DON'T MAKE ME EMBARRASS YOU IN FRONT OF COMPANY.
WHY ARE YOU MAKING SUCH A BIG DEAL OUT OF THIS?
WHY AREN'T YOU?
HONEY. YOU CAN'T KEEP RUNNING AWAY FROM THINGS.
I KNOW YOU'RE STRONG AND HEALTHY UP HERE.
I NEED YOU TO BE STRONG AND HEALTHY IN HERE.
WILL YOU COME TO THE SUPPORT GROUP WITH ME? JUST ONCE?
...
MAYBE.

I'M NOT LETTING THIS GO. XAVIER, YOU'RE WELCOME TO STAY FOR DINNER IF YOU CAN TOLERATE MY DAUGHTER'S HORRIBLE MANNERS.
YES, MA'AM. THANK YOU, MISS RONNIE.
LET'S GET BACK TO THIS. SO OUR APPROACH HERE SHOULD BE--
HOLD UP. ISN'T YOUR MOMS DOING WHAT PEOPLE ARE SUPPOSED TO DO WHEN THEY LOVE YOU? CHECK *UP* ON YOU?
I GUESS.
AND WHAT'S GOING ON WITH YOU AND THE CHAMPIONS? SHOULDN'T **THEY** BE HELPING YOU INSTEAD OF REGULAR, DEGULAR, SHMEGULAR ME?
THINGS WITH THE CHAMPIONS ARE... **AWKWARD** RIGHT NOW. DO WE HAVE TO TALK ABOUT THIS?
YOU'LL DO JUST FINE. ESPECIALLY IF YOU CAN HELP ME FIGURE THIS OUT.
OKAY.
BUT ONLY BECAUSE YOUR MOM IS MAKING DINNER.
TWO HOURS LATER...
MAYBE THERE *ISN'T* A PATTERN. MAYBE PEOPLE JUST LIKE TO STEAL PHONES.
NO PATTERN.
NADA.
TOTALLY RANDOM.
LET'S JUST REVIEW WHAT WE KNOW. VICTIMS' AGES?
RACE?
NEIGHBORHOOD?
DINNER IS ALMOST READY! Y'ALL DONE WORKING?
YES!
NO!
YES, THIS IS RIRI! WE ARE DEFINITIVELY AFFIRMATIVELY DONE WORKING! TASK COMPLETE!
I DON'T EVEN TALK LIKE THAT. I-- *WAIT!*

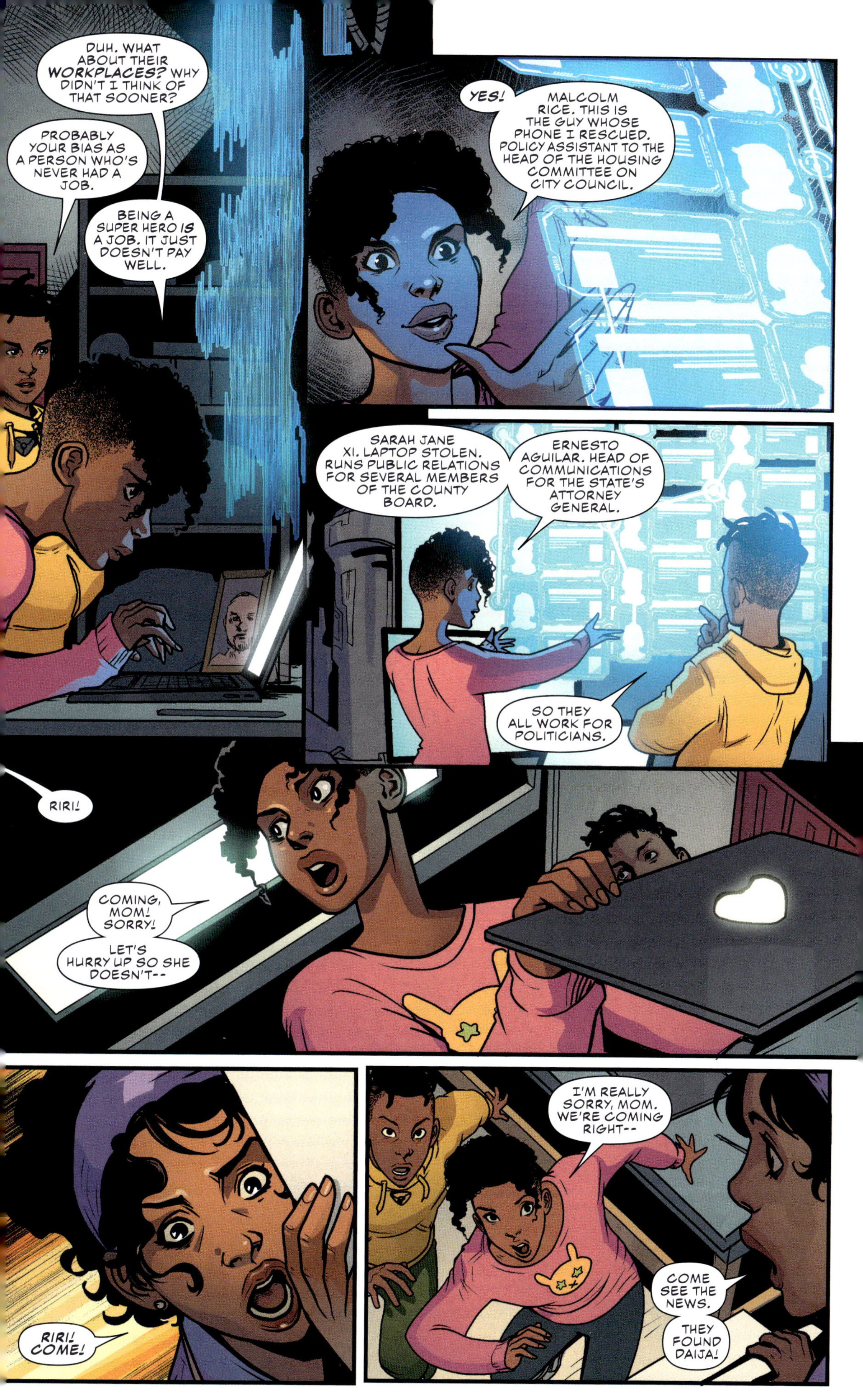
DUH. WHAT ABOUT THEIR WORKPLACES? WHY DIDN'T I THINK OF THAT SOONER?
PROBABLY YOUR BIAS AS A PERSON WHO'S NEVER HAD A JOB.
BEING A SUPER HERO IS A JOB. IT JUST DOESN'T PAY WELL.
YES!
MALCOLM RICE. THIS IS THE GUY WHOSE PHONE I RESCUED. POLICY ASSISTANT TO THE HEAD OF THE HOUSING COMMITTEE ON CITY COUNCIL.
SARAH JANE XI. LAPTOP STOLEN. RUNS PUBLIC RELATIONS FOR SEVERAL MEMBERS OF THE COUNTY BOARD.
ERNESTO AGUILAR. HEAD OF COMMUNICATIONS FOR THE STATE'S ATTORNEY GENERAL.
SO THEY ALL WORK FOR POLITICIANS.
RIRI!
COMING, MOM! SORRY!
LET'S HURRY UP SO SHE DOESN'T--
RIRI! COME!
I'M REALLY SORRY, MOM. WE'RE COMING RIGHT--
COME SEE THE NEWS.
THEY FOUND DAIJA!

I FELT...STRESS. AND ANXIETY. SO, I...I RAN AWAY FROM HOME.
TV3
SHE LOOKS... OFF.
TV3
I...TRIPPED OVER A BRANCH IN A WOODED AREA JUST OUTSIDE OF THE CITY. I WAS KNOCKED UNCONSCIOUS.
TV3
TOO MANY MENTAL HEALTH ISSUES AMONG YOUNG PEOPLE THESE DAYS.
SOUNDS LIKE AN EXCUSE. HER PARENTS SHOULD BE IN JAIL.
HOW DO WE KNOW SHE WASN'T UNDER THE INFLUENCE OF ILLEGAL SUBSTANCES?
BIRCH RUNS UNOPPOSED AS KEY OPPONENT DROPS FROM GOVERNOR'S RACE. TORNADO WATCH IN DEKALB
WOW. GREAT TO KNOW THAT IF WE EVER WENT MISSING, THIS IS HOW THEY'D TREAT US.
I DON'T KNOW. THIS STORY LEAVES ME WITH A WHOLE LOT OF QUESTIONS.
ME TOO.
AND I'M GONNA GET SOME ANSWERS.

TAP TAP

IT'S A SEALED WINDOW! IT DOESN'T OPEN! I CAN'T--

VZZZZ

OH, LORD.

OW.

WHY ARE YOU DOING THIS?

I COULD ASK YOU THE SAME QUESTION. WHY ARE YOU ON TV TELLING LIES?

"YOU'RE CALLING ME A LIAR?

YOU CAN TELL ME THE TRUTH! I'M NOT A LITTLE KID ANYMORE."

"OBVIOUSLY! YOU'RE A GROWN PERSON WITH HER OWN LIFE.

AND WAY TOO MUCH 'I'M THE ONE WHO MADE IT OUT THE HOOD' SURVIVOR'S GUILT AND NOT ENOUGH COMMON SENSE."

"OH, IT'S LIKE THAT?"

"IT'S LIKE THAT!"

"I'LL LEAVE YOU TO SOLVE YOUR OWN PROBLEMS, THEN.

WHAT ARE THOSE, THE RETRO FLYGIRL EIGHTS?"

"YOU A SNEAKERHEAD NOW?"

"I'M JUST CURIOUS."

"LEAVE, RIRI."

"I'M GONE."

"I KNEW THIS WOULD HAPPEN."

LEAVE HER ALONE. SHE'S NOT COMING BACK.
YOU TOLD ME THAT IF I LET YOU GO, HER INTEREST WOULD WANE. YOU WERE WRONG.
AND SHE WILL PAY FOR YOUR ERROR WITH HER LIFE!
NOOOOOOOO!!!
DAIJA?
DAIJA! WERE YOU TALKING?
NO ONE IS HERE, SWEETIE. YOU'RE SAFE. IT'S OKAY. YOU'RE OKAY.
NO. NO NO NO NO NO...

YOU'RE OKAY, I PROMISE.
NO.
WHO WAS THAT PERSON?
WHOEVER HE WAS, HE'S AFTER YOU. YOU'RE LUCKY HE DIDN'T CATCH YOU PUTTING A BUG IN THAT SHOE.
HOW'D HE GET PAST THE NURSE?
SURELY SHE IS CLOSE.
A TENACIOUS ONE. AND QUICK.
IDEALISTIC. SHE CONJURES MEMORIES OF ANOTHER ARMORED WARRIOR I ONCE KNEW.
THOUGH SHE BEARS, IN HER EYES, A DARKNESS HE DID NOT HAVE.
VSSH
WHATEVER POSSIBILITY LIES IN HER BROKEN HEART IS AS DANGEROUS TO ME AS IT IS PROMISING.

YOU MAY HAVE YOUR MYSTICAL WHATEVER NINJA POWERS.
BUT I HAVE THERMAL IMAGING.
AND YOU'RE NOT GOING ANYWHERE.
CHILD, YOU HAVEN'T ANY UNDERSTANDING--
--OF THE TYPE OF POWER YOU'RE DEALING WITH.
KRASH

GET--
--OFF ME!
I CAN'T SEE HIM!
HE'S BLOCKING IT SOMEHOW.
THERMAL IMAGING ENGAGED!
DON'T PANIC. WE'LL--
AAAAAAH!
YOU CANNOT HIDE FROM ME.
LET THAT BE THE LAST LESSON YOU LEARN IN THIS LIFE.
D-DORSAL! DORSAL ROCKET!

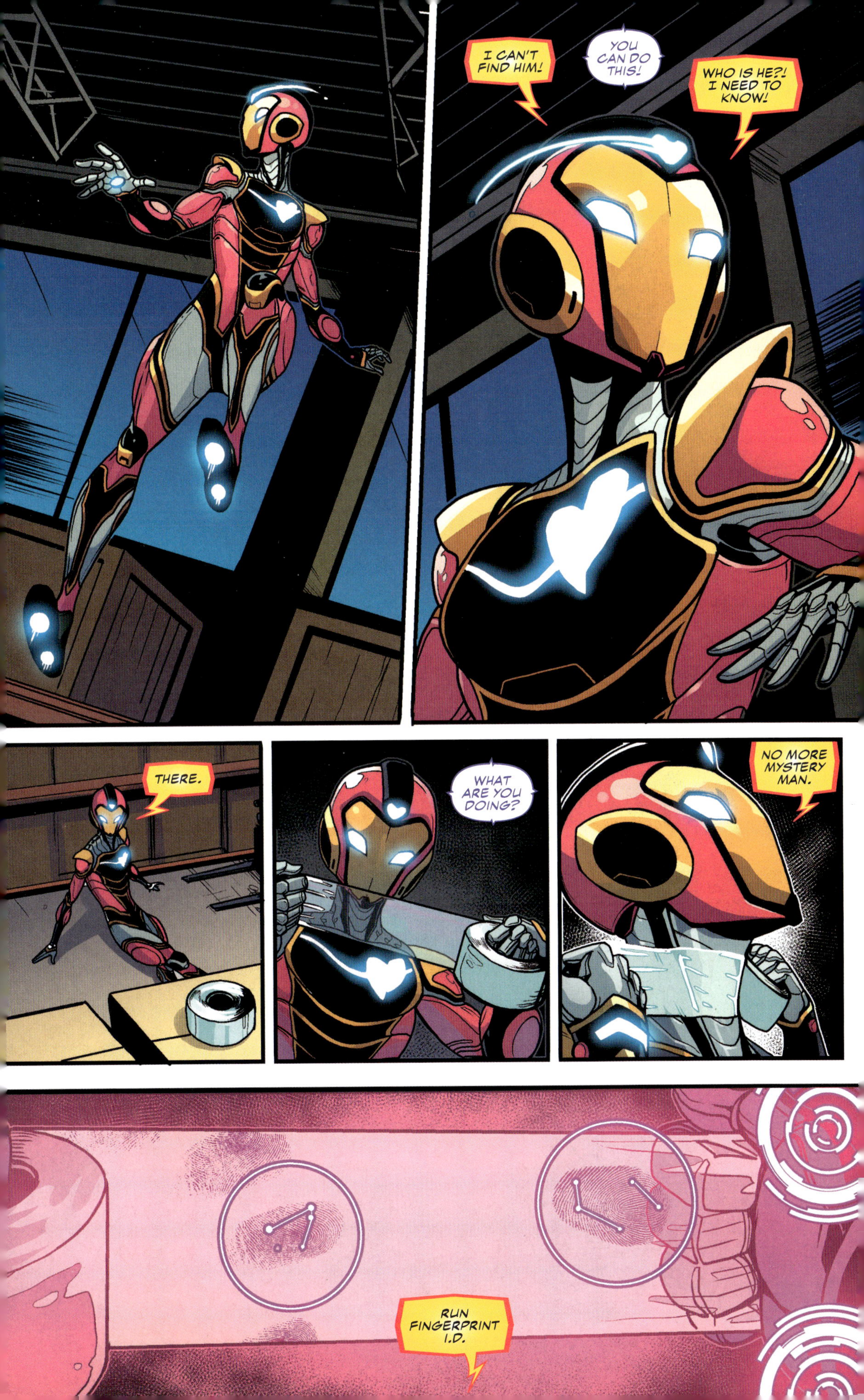
I CAN'T FIND HIM!
YOU CAN DO THIS!
WHO IS HE?! I NEED TO KNOW!
THERE.
WHAT ARE YOU DOING?
NO MORE MYSTERY MAN.
RUN FINGERPRINT I.D.

MIDNIGHT'S FIRE. MASTER THIEF. EXPERT MARTIAL ARTIST. MAGICAL ABILITY. SUPERIOR AGILITY. SUPERIOR STRENGTH. EXTRASENSORY PERCEPTION.
OH MY GOD.
DO YOU SEE NOW HOW FOOLISH YOU ARE TO RESIST?
ACK!
DWELL IN YOUR FEAR.
COME BACK, RIRI, COME BACK! THANOS DIDN'T KILL YOU.
YOU AND THE CHAMPIONS ESCAPED!
YOU LIVED. YOU LIVED! COME BACK!
COME BACK TO ME, GIRL! COME ON!

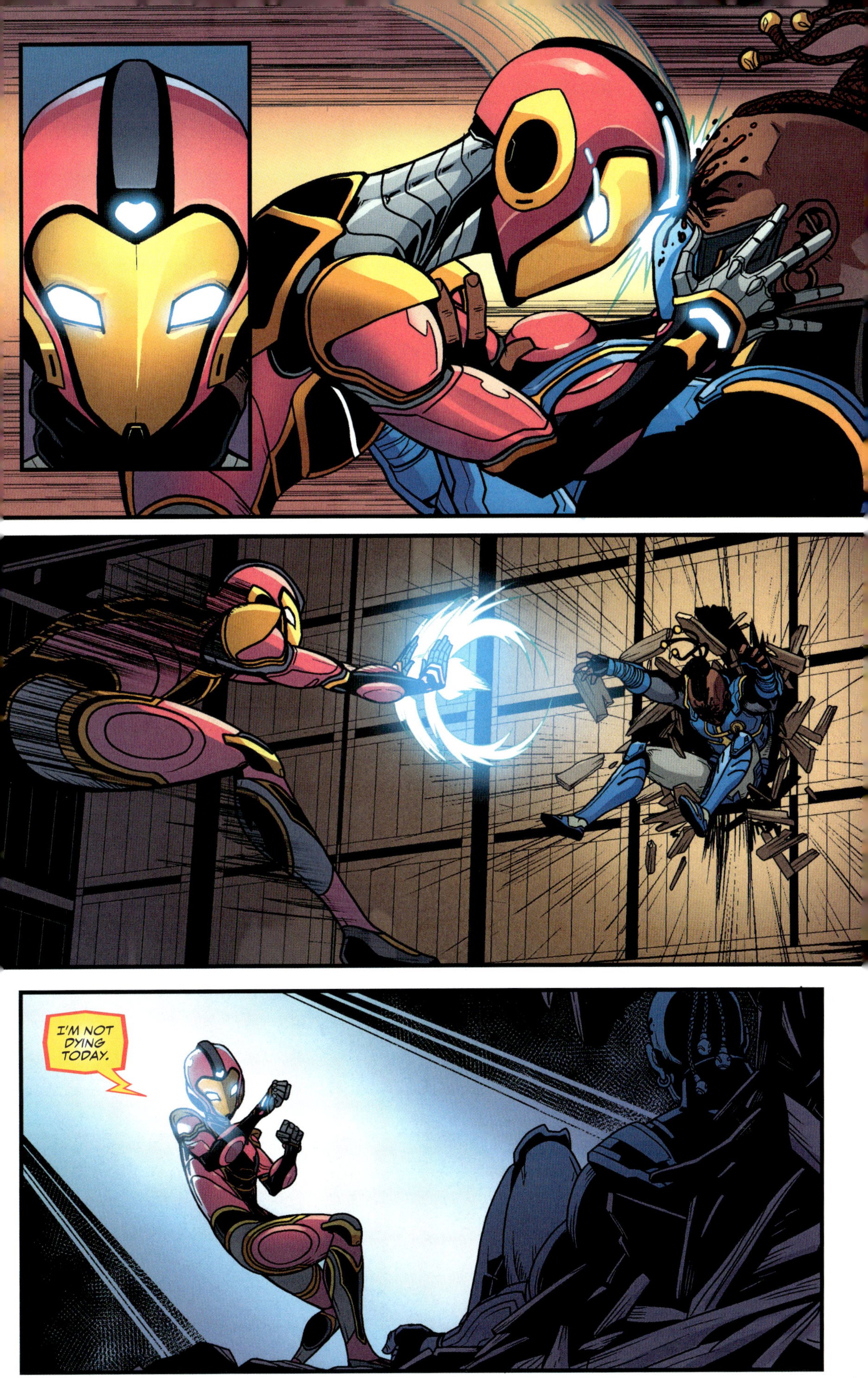
I'M NOT DYING TODAY.

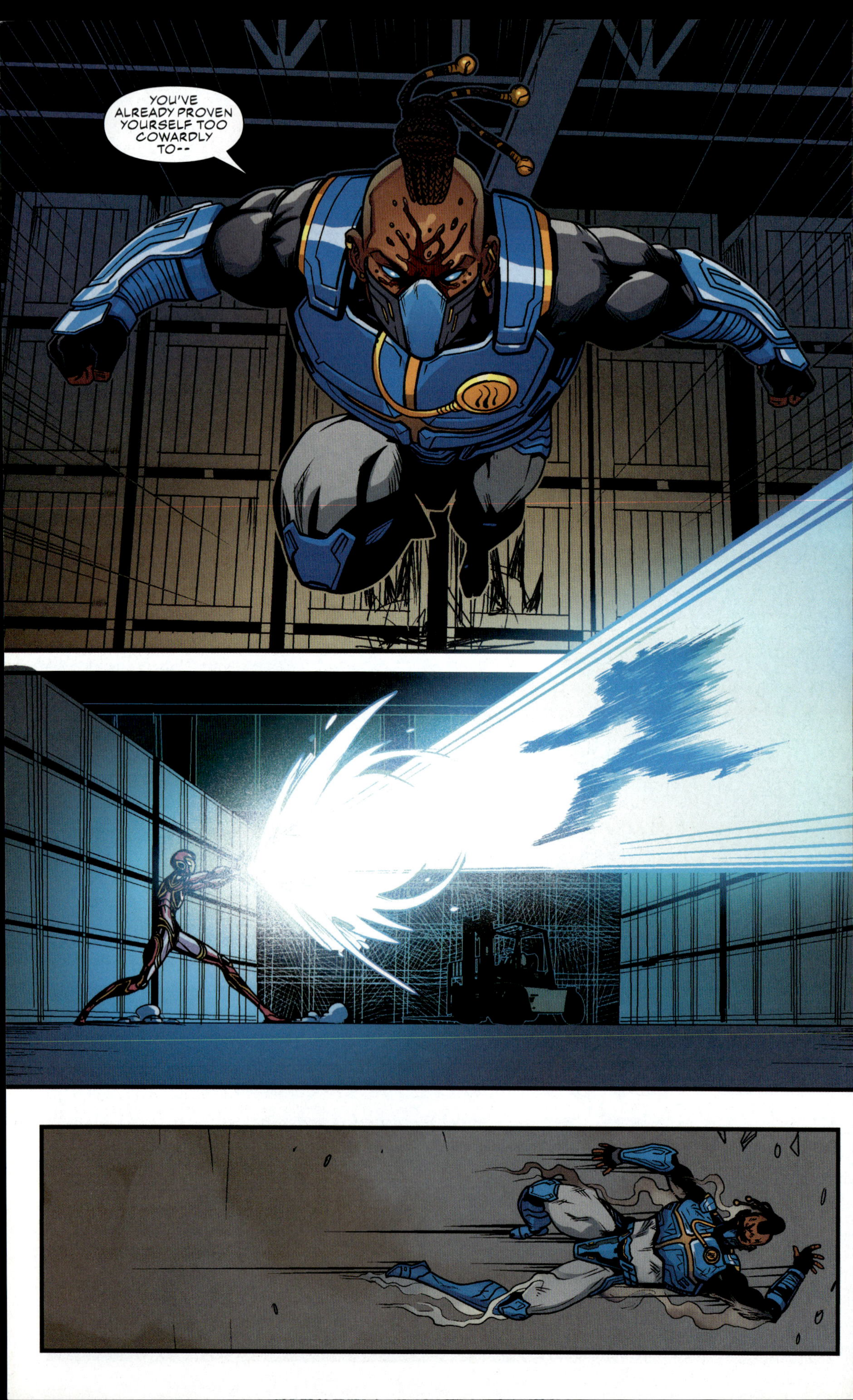
YOU'VE ALREADY PROVEN YOURSELF TOO COWARDLY TO--

LET'S CALL... SOMEBODY. THE AUTHORITIES. AND GET OUT OF HERE.

"DEATH IS ALSO A SEEKER. FOREVER SEEKING ME."

DISTURBANCE IN A WAREHOUSE NEAR CENTRAL AND HARRISON. SOME KIND OF EXPLOSION. DISPATCHING NEARBY UNITS.

COPS ARE COMING. LET'S GO, N.A.T.A.L.I.E.

SHOULDN'T WE STAY? BY MY READING, HE'S NOT DEAD. HE'LL DISAPPEAR BEFORE THEY GET HERE.

RIRI.
RIRI!
WHAT?!
YOU STORMED OUT OF THE HOUSE LOOKING FOR TROUBLE, WITH NO PLAN, AND YOU ALMOST DIED. AGAIN.
YOU NEED PROFESSIONAL HELP--YOU NEED CHAMPIONS HELP! YOU NEED--
I NEED TO FIGURE OUT WHAT HAPPENED TO DAIJA! I NEED TO ACT LIKE A HERO AND HANDLE MY BUSINESS!
I NEED TO STOP BEING RULED BY FEAR!
SO YOUR MOTHER DESERVES TO LOSE SOMEONE AGAIN BECAUSE YOU'RE PRIDEFUL?
HOW MANY PEOPLE HAVE TO DIE, RIRI?
LISTEN. I'M SORRY. I JUST--
DEACTIVATE.
NO!

"I JUST NEED TO BE ALONE." "DEACTIVATE. TWO-HOUR UPDATE CYCLE. RUN ROUTINE MAINTENANCE."

"AFFIRMATIVE."

"BEING ALONE IS THE BEST WAY TO MAKE SURE YOU DON'T LET ANYBODY DOWN."

"THAT'S WHY I FLY SOLO."

"POLICE!"

"THERE'S... THERE'S NO ONE HERE."

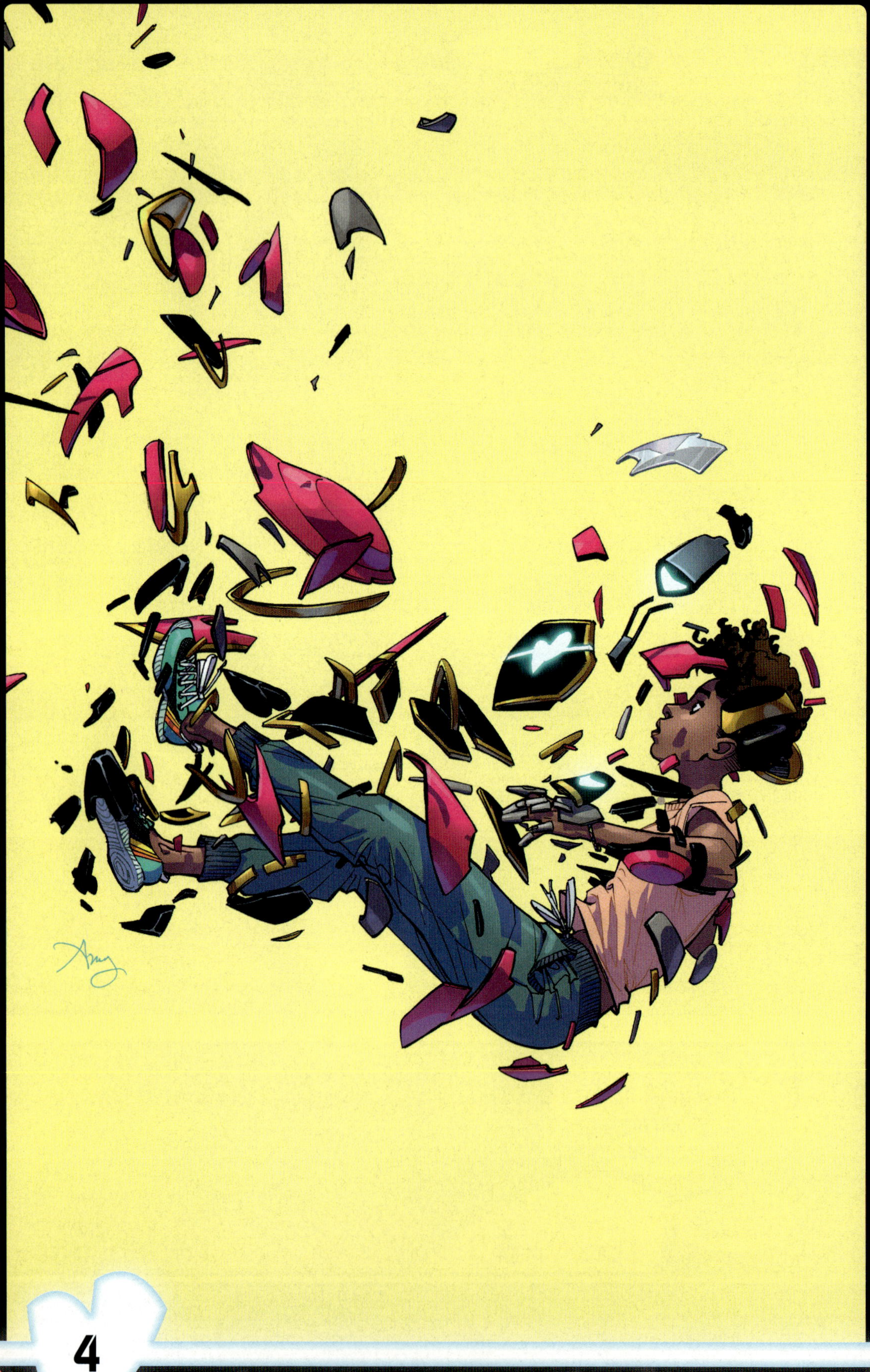

TRAINING SEQUENCE INTERRUPTED. RIRI, YOU HAVE A CALL.

≶HUFF≷ HELLO?

MS. WILLIAMS! HOW THE HECK ARE YOU?
DEAN BRYANT. I'M GOOD. YOU?
GOOD. I'M HERE WITH SOME VERY IMPORTANT DONORS WHO WANT TO MEET YOU. THEY CAME A LONG WAY TO MEET M.I.T.'S ONE AND ONLY IRONHEART!
BUT I CAN'T HELP BUT NOTICE...
...YOU'RE NOT HERE.
AH. YES. WELL, YOU SEE, I'M ON SORT OF A...REMOTE...GLOBAL LEARNING... EXCURSION. OFF-SITE. YOU KNOW M.I.T. STUDENTS. THE WORLD IS OUR LABORATORY!
YES, WELL, THESE DONORS AND THE TRUSTEES--
YOU KNOW WHAT, DEAN BRYANT, SO SORRY, BUT MY MOM NEEDS ME. THANKS FOR CHECKING IN.
BUT I--
BOOP
OH! YOU ARE...ACTUALLY STANDING THERE. I GUESS I DESERVE THAT, HUH?
ASK AND YOU SHALL RECEIVE.
CAN I TALK TO MY DAUGHTER FOR A SECOND? WITHOUT THE SUIT?

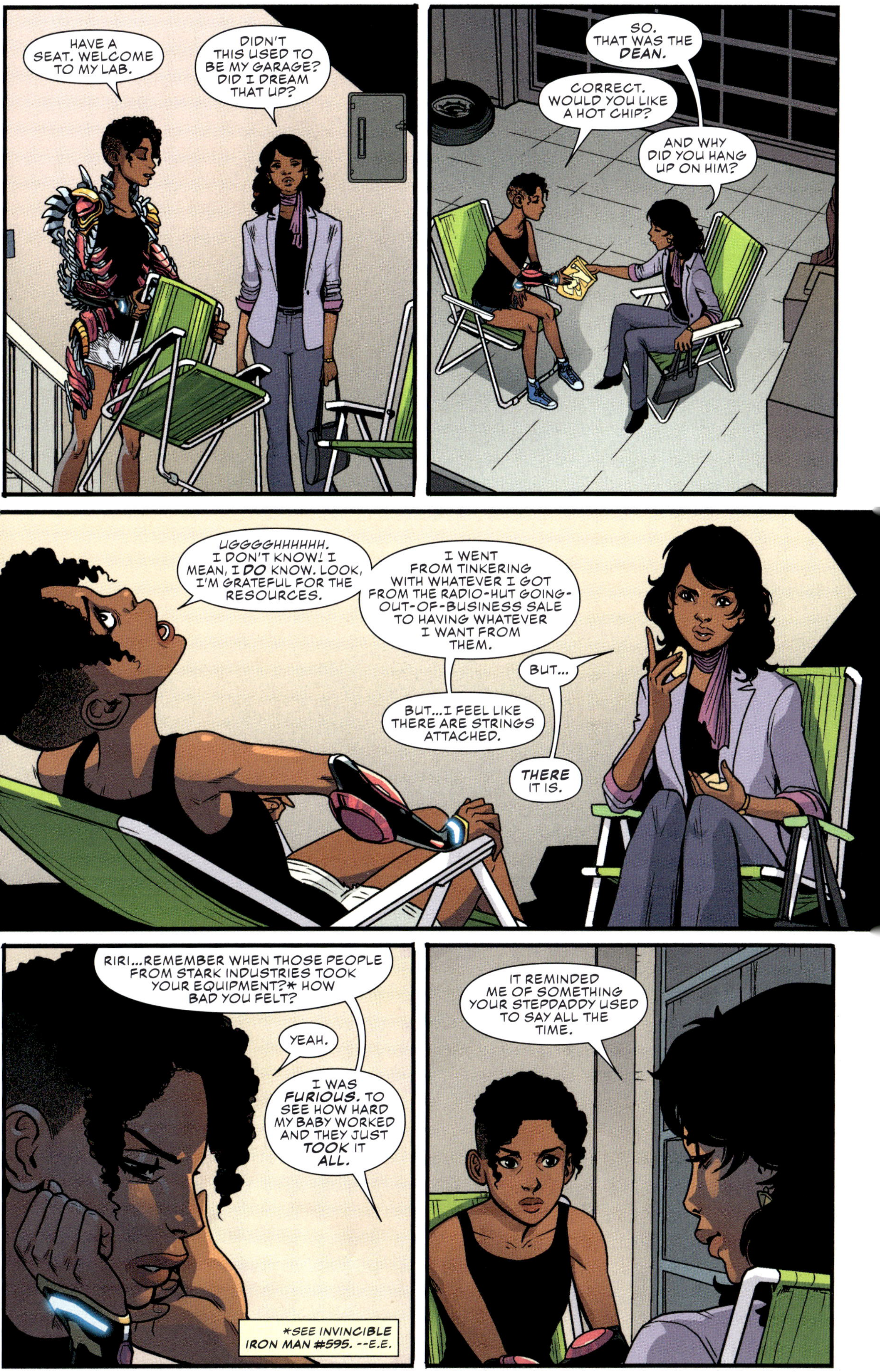
HAVE A SEAT. WELCOME TO MY LAB.
DIDN'T THIS USED TO BE MY GARAGE? DID I DREAM THAT UP?
SO. THAT WAS THE DEAN.
CORRECT. WOULD YOU LIKE A HOT CHIP?
AND WHY DID YOU HANG UP ON HIM?
UGGGGHHHHHH. I DON'T KNOW! I MEAN, I DO KNOW. LOOK, I'M GRATEFUL FOR THE RESOURCES.
I WENT FROM TINKERING WITH WHATEVER I GOT FROM THE RADIO-HUT GOING-OUT-OF-BUSINESS SALE TO HAVING WHATEVER I WANT FROM THEM.
BUT...
BUT...I FEEL LIKE THERE ARE STRINGS ATTACHED.
THERE IT IS.
RIRI...REMEMBER WHEN THOSE PEOPLE FROM STARK INDUSTRIES TOOK YOUR EQUIPMENT?* HOW BAD YOU FELT?
YEAH.
I WAS FURIOUS. TO SEE HOW HARD MY BABY WORKED AND THEY JUST TOOK IT ALL.
*SEE INVINCIBLE IRON MAN #595. --E.E.
IT REMINDED ME OF SOMETHING YOUR STEPDADDY USED TO SAY ALL THE TIME.

"GARY WANTED TO *OWN* EVERYTHING. THIS HOUSE. AND THAT OLD HOOPTIE HE BOUGHT BECAUSE HE COULD PAY FOR IT IN CASH WITHOUT A CAR NOTE."

"EVEN THAT AUTO SHOP HE RAN FOR A WHILE--HE OWNED THAT. REMEMBER? OVER THERE ON 75TH AND BLACKSTONE?"

"YOU USED TO BE THERE EVERY DAY WHEN WE COULDN'T AFFORD DAY CARE."

"HE ALWAYS BELIEVED WE SHOULD OWN WHAT WE COULD. IF NOT, ANYTHING WE HAD COULD BE TAKEN AWAY. SOMETIMES I THOUGHT HE WAS PARANOID."

"BUT WHEN THEY CAME FOR YOUR *SUIT*..."

...I GUESS WHAT I'M TRYING TO SAY IS...SOMETIMES IT'S NICE TO NOT OWE *NOBODY*. YOU UNDERSTAND?

YEAH.

MOM? YOU SAID "STEPDADDY." BUT...

...YOU KNOW HE WAS THE ONLY FATHER I EVER KNEW. RIGHT? HE WAS MY FATHER.

OH, HONEY...I... I KNOW.

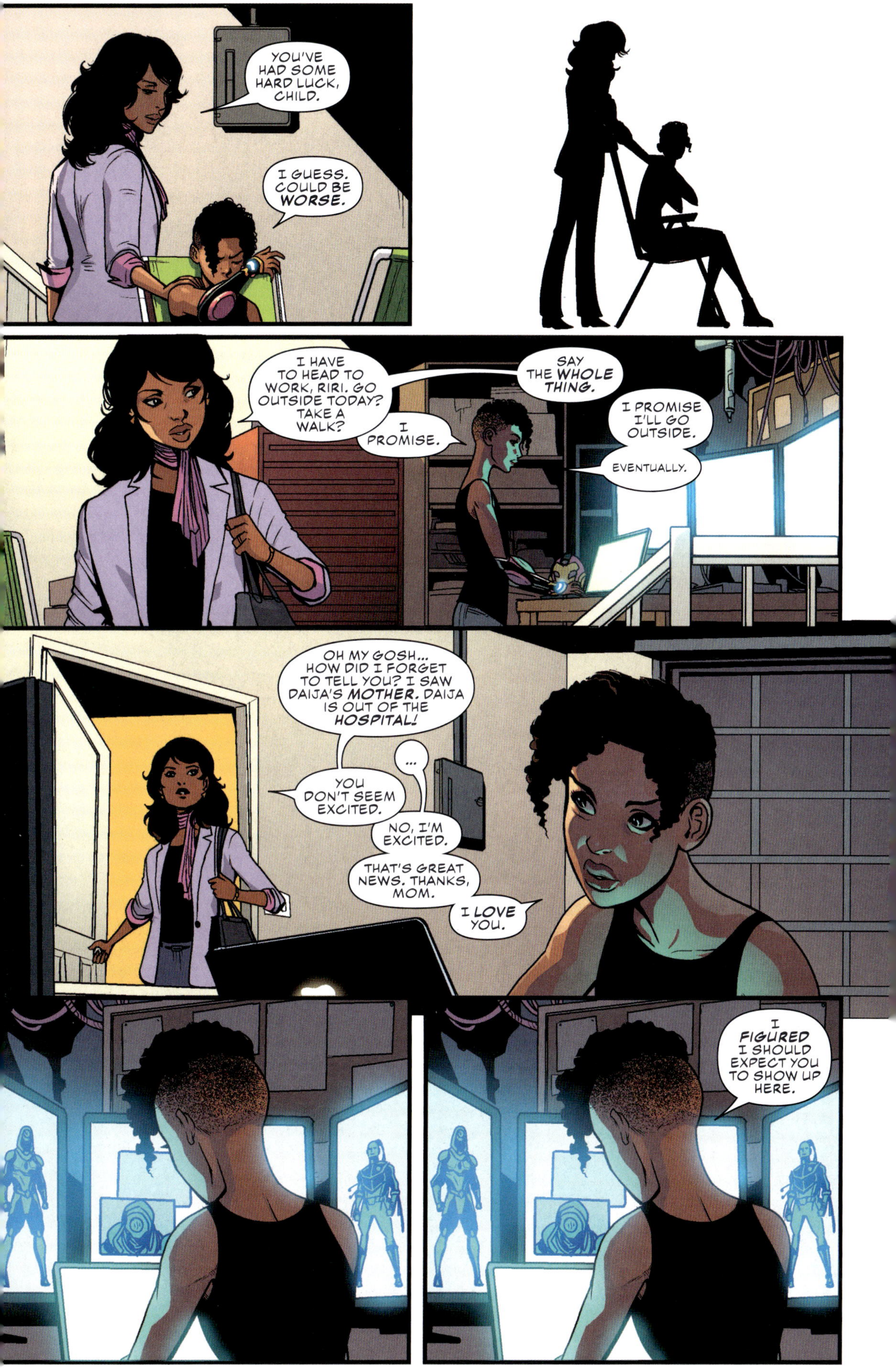
YOU'VE HAD SOME HARD LUCK, CHILD.
I GUESS. COULD BE WORSE.
I HAVE TO HEAD TO WORK, RIRI. GO OUTSIDE TODAY? TAKE A WALK?
I PROMISE.
SAY THE WHOLE THING.
I PROMISE I'LL GO OUTSIDE.
EVENTUALLY.
OH MY GOSH... HOW DID I FORGET TO TELL YOU? I SAW DAIJA'S MOTHER. DAIJA IS OUT OF THE HOSPITAL!
...
YOU DON'T SEEM EXCITED.
NO, I'M EXCITED.
THAT'S GREAT NEWS. THANKS, MOM.
I LOVE YOU.
I FIGURED I SHOULD EXPECT YOU TO SHOW UP HERE.

MAY I ENTER?
WHAT ARE YOU, A VAMPIRE? YEAH, COME IN.
IF YOU FORESAW MY ARRIVAL, WHY DID YOU NOT TRY TO STOP ME? ARE YOU NOT AFRAID?
DO YOU WANT A POP?
NOT A POP GUY, HUH?
MIDNIGHT'S FIRE, YOU ALMOST KILLED ME. BUT YOU DIDN'T. AND I DON'T HAVE A SECRET IDENTITY. SO I FIGURED YOU'D BE BACK, AND IT'D BE THE END OF ME, OR IT WOULDN'T. PLUS...
...I THOUGHT YOU MIGHT WANT TO TALK ABOUT THIS.

SO, IT IS AS I SUSPECTED.
THE SIGN OF THE TEN RINGS. YOU HAVE SEEN IT. AND IT *TEMPTS* YOU.
I DID SOME RESEARCH. NOT THAT THERE'S MUCH TO FIND. YOU ALL ARE GOOD AT COVERING YOUR TRACKS.
A SKILL IN WHICH WE SPECIALIZE AND *EXCEL.*
A TERRORIST GROUP SO COVERT THAT SOME PEOPLE THINK IT'S A *MYTH.* NO KNOWN POLITICAL AGENDA. NO REGIONAL FOCUS OR CENTER OF OPERATIONS.
I *SEE.* SO IN OTHER WORDS...
...YOU KNOW NOTHING. AND YOU, RIRI WILLIAMS, THIRST *INFINITELY* FOR KNOWLEDGE. SO PERMIT ME TO OFFER IT.

CAMBODIA.
MANY YEARS AGO.

"I CANNOT TELL YOU ABOUT THE TEN RINGS WITHOUT TELLING YOU WHO I AM.

"AND I CANNOT TELL YOU WHO I AM WITHOUT TELLING YOU WHO MY FATHER WAS.

"OUR FATHERS' STORIES ARE OUR OWN. WHETHER WE NAME THEM OR NOT. WHETHER WE KNOW THEM OR NOT.

"IN US, THEY LIVE.

"THEY SHAPE OUR DESTINY, IN WAYS SEEN AND UNSEEN.

"MY FATHER WAS A SOLDIER.

"HIS TRAVELS BROUGHT HIM TO SOMETHING FAR MORE POWERFUL THAN THE EMPIRES OF MEN.

"MY GRANDMOTHER, TAI, WAS A *RUTHLESS* MASTER STRATEGIST. AND ON THAT DAY, SHE MADE A PACT WITH MY FATHER AND HIS MEN.

"IF EACH OF THEM MARRIED ONE OF HER ACOLYTES, TAI PROMISED THEM *UNLIMITED WEALTH AND POWER.*

"HOW DEHUMANIZING, TO TRADE IN HUMAN LOVE. BUT THE MEN WERE GREEDY, SPELLBOUND OR BOTH.

"TWINS! WHAT A BLESSING!"

"Y-YES..."

"TAI DID NOT ONLY DEMAND THEIR *HEARTS.* SHE DEMANDED THEIR *CHILDREN.*

"SHE BELIEVED THAT WE WOULD POSSESS UNIMAGINABLE POWER--THAT SHE COULD *CONTROL.*

"MY MOTHER WANTED SOMETHING ELSE FOR US. SOMETHING OF *OUR* CHOOSING.

"THANK YOU."

"THEY WILL HAVE A HARD LIFE HERE. BUT THEY WILL *LIVE.*"

"AFTER THAT, THE STREETS RAISED ME.

THIS IS CONCRETE DRAGONS TERRITORY. IS THAT UNDERSTOOD?
"AT FIRST, I WAS TOO SMALL-MINDED. I LACKED DISCIPLINE.
PLEASE. I'M SORRY. IT WAS ALL A MISUNDERSTANDING, I SWEAR.
THEN YOUR MIND IS WEAK.
"ALTHOUGH I POSSESSED ABILITIES BEYOND THOSE OF ORDINARY MEN, I BARELY KNEW HOW TO MARSHAL THEM.
"STILL, AS MY POWER GREW IN THE UNDERWORLD, IN THE STREETS...
"...I WAS RESTLESS. UNSATISFIED.
"MY POWER WAS MUCH BIGGER THAN MYSELF.
"I COULD NEVER ESCAPE THE DESTINY SET BEFORE ME BY MY FATHER.
"THE PACT HAS NEVER BEEN FULFILLED. ITS PROMISE REMAINS.

"I HAVE HONED MY ABILITIES. PREPARED MYSELF.

"I AM PALADIN AND MERCENARY.

"A FIRE THAT BURNS AT MIDNIGHT. TO A COLD MAN SEARCHING FOR WARMTH, AN ILLUSION. A *TRICK* OF THE *MIND*.

"TO A MAN BELIEVING HE IS SAFE, A *TERROR*.

"NOW I AM READY TO FULFILL A *PROMISE* MADE TO THE UNIVERSE.

"MY FATHER AND GRANDMOTHER THOUGHT OUR DESTINY COULD BE FULFILLED AS *INDIVIDUALS*.

"BUT POWER WITHOUT STRUCTURE IS CHAOS."

THE SANCTUM SANCTORUM.
NEW YORK CITY.
SEVERAL YEARS AGO.

"YOU SEE, THE *TEMPLE* OF TAI WAS BUT *ONE* PORTAL TO SOMETHING *GRAND*.

"COSMIC *ENERGY* SURPASSING HUMAN COMPREHENSION. WITH CONDUITS ACROSS OUR WORLD AND BEYOND.

"THE SOURCE OF MY *OWN* ABILITIES, AS WELL AS THOSE OF MANY OTHERS.

"THE *WELLSPRING* OF POWER!

"MOST BELIEVE THAT ALL ITS EARTHLY PORTALS WERE SEALED.

"I BELIEVE THERE IS ANOTHER *UNDETECTED* CONDUIT TO THE WELLSPRING. AND I AIM TO FIND AND CONTROL IT."

...YOU ARE SILENT.

THIS IS A LOT.

THIS WELLSPRING. IS IT IN CHICAGO?

I DO NOT KNOW.

THEN WHY ARE YOU HERE?

THE WELLSPRING IS MY GOAL. BUT TEN RINGS HAS ITS OWN PREROGATIVE.

TO SEIZE AS MANY WEAPONS AS WE CAN.

BUT WHY? FOR WHAT?

THE SWORD. THE BOW. THE GUN.

FROM THE SAMURAI TO THE KNIGHT, GREAT WARRIORS KNOW THAT THE WEAPON IS NOT MERELY A TOOL. THE WEAPON HAS A SPIRIT.

A TEN RINGS WARRIOR KNOWS THAT TO GATHER WEAPONS...THIS, IN ITSELF, IS A SPIRITUAL PURSUIT.

YOU WANT TO HOARD WEAPONS JUST TO HAVE THEM? YOU DON'T EVEN BELIEVE IN ANYTHING?!

WE DO BELIEVE. WE VERY MUCH BELIEVE.

THE WEAPON IS OUR GOD.

AND I AM HERE TO INVITE YOU, RIRI WILLIAMS, TO COME WORSHIP WITH US.

WE ARE AN ANCIENT ORDER. AND WE GATHER UNIMAGINABLE POWER. POWER THAT I WOULD LIKE YOU, IN TIME, TO UNDERSTAND.

"THE STRENGTH OF THE *TEN RINGS.* AND SOON, THE COSMIC ENERGY OF THE *WELLSPRING OF POWER.*

"YOU ARE YOUNG, BUT A SKILLED TACTICIAN. IMAGINE... YOUR *BRILLIANCE* MATCHED WITH *UNPARALLELED POWER.*

"AND AS MY FATHER PLANTED THE SEEDS FOR MY FATE, I WILL BE AS A FATHER TO YOU.

"THE PACT WILL BE FULFILLED AT LAST THROUGH *YOU*, MY CHOSEN HEIR.

"TOGETHER, WE CAN BRING *ORDER* TO A CHAOTIC WORLD."

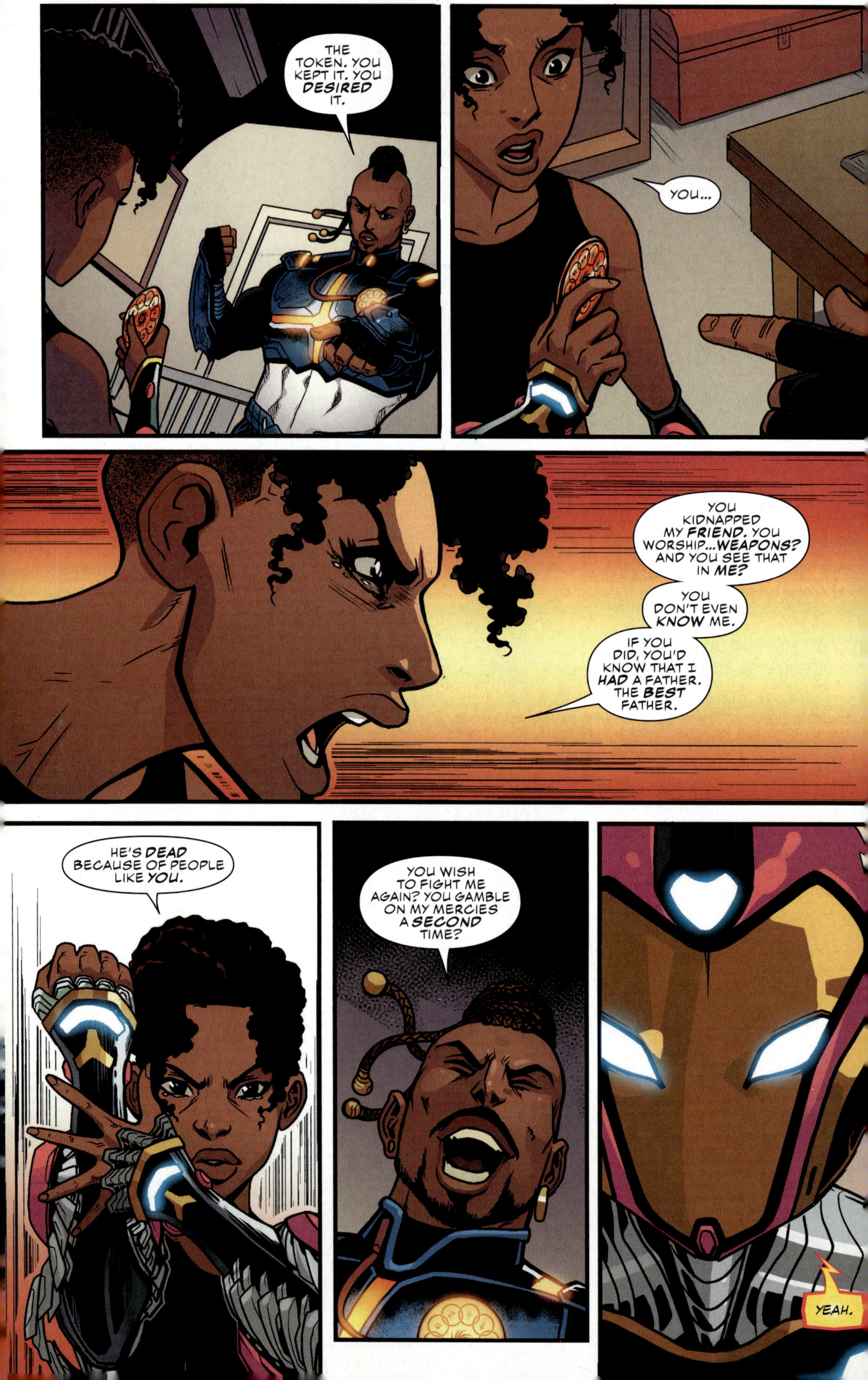
THE TOKEN. YOU KEPT IT. YOU DESIRED IT.
YOU...
YOU KIDNAPPED MY FRIEND. YOU WORSHIP...WEAPONS? AND YOU SEE THAT IN ME?
YOU DON'T EVEN KNOW ME.
IF YOU DID, YOU'D KNOW THAT I HAD A FATHER. THE BEST FATHER.
HE'S DEAD BECAUSE OF PEOPLE LIKE YOU.
YOU WISH TO FIGHT ME AGAIN? YOU GAMBLE ON MY MERCIES A SECOND TIME?
YEAH.

RRRRAHHHH!
YOU SAID I KNEW NOTHING ABOUT THE TEN RINGS. THEN TELL ME EVERYTHING YOU HAVE PLANNED.
RIRI, STOP AND THINK!
I WANT ANSWERS!
N.A.T.A.L.I.E., ENHANCE PALMAR GRIP.

"WHO DO YOU WORK WITH? WHO TOOK DAIJA? WHY WON'T YOU LEAVE ME ALONE?"

LISTEN TO ME.
YOU CONCEAL YOUR TRUE SELF, YOUNG ONE!
N.A.T.A.L.I.E., DRONE PROTOTYPE!
IT HASN'T BEEN TESTED! IT--
DO IT!
AAAAAARGH!
ENOUGH.

I WON'T KILL YOU TODAY, RIRI WILLIAMS.
BECAUSE I SEE YOU. YOUR AWE IN THE FACE OF STRENGTH. LIKE ME YOU WORSHIP IT. PERHAPS YOU ARE TOO YOUNG TO KNOW. BUT I SEE IT.
SLEEP.
PERHAPS, AS I DO, YOU WILL FIND CLARITY...
...IN DARKNESS.

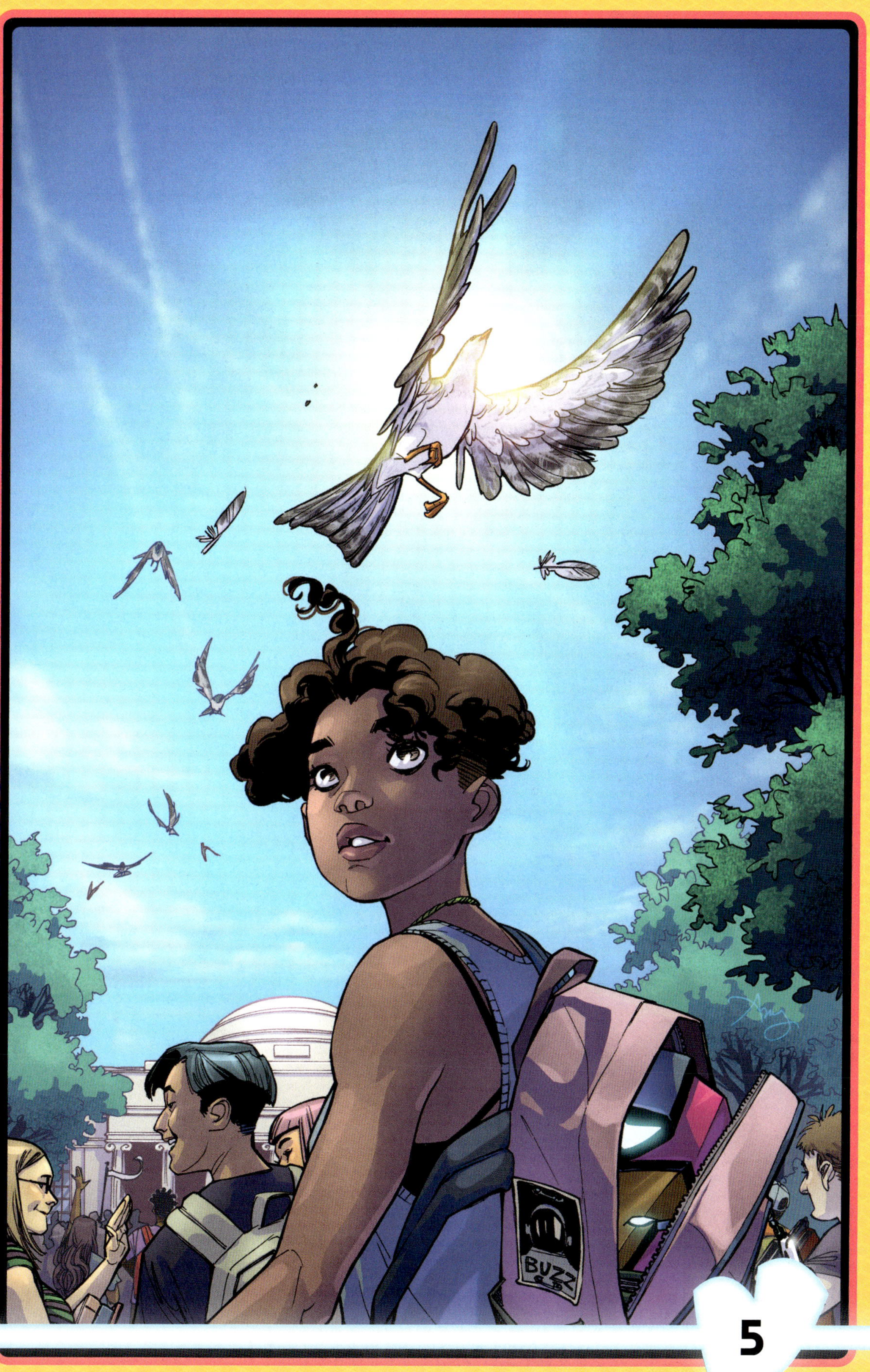
BUZZ

CHICAGO.

I LIVE IN A CITY THAT PEOPLE CALL DANGEROUS.

AND IT IS, I GUESS.

PEOPLE USED TO CALL US THE "HOG BUTCHER FOR THE WORLD."

AND IF WE HAVE TO BE THE BOGEYMAN...

...THE PLACE THAT MAKES OTHER PEOPLE FEEL GOOD ABOUT WHERE THEY LAY THEIR HEADS AT NIGHT...

...SO BE IT.

PEOPLE HERE ARE STRUGGLING TO SURVIVE.

AND A WISE PERSON ONCE TOLD ME THAT THE BUSINESS OF SURVIVAL AIN'T ALWAYS PRETTY.

THANKS FOR HELPING ME, XAVIER. I NEED TO GET EVERYTHING BACK TO NORMAL IN HERE, BUT MIDNIGHT'S FIRE MADE A MESS.
ALL GOOD. WHAT DID YOU TELL YOUR MOMS?
THAT I WAS TESTING A NEW MOTION-SENSOR SYSTEM IN HERE AND NOT TO COME IN.
SO WHAT'S THE NEXT MOVE?
I'M THINKING OF RUNNING SOME SURVEILLANCE ON DAIJA. FOLLOW HER AND SEE WHAT'S REALLY GOING ON.
YOU'RE GONNA DO WHAT?! FIRST OF ALL, THAT'S INTRUSIVE.
AND LOOK AT YOU! YOU'RE ALL BEAT UP! MIDNIGHT'S FIRE ATTACKED YOU--
WOULD YOU KEEP IT DOWN?
HE ATTACKED YOU AND LEFT YOU UNCONSCIOUS IN YOUR OWN GARAGE.
HE'S DANGEROUS.
SHHH! HUSH. I DON'T WANT MY MOM TO KNOW WHAT HAPPENED.
LOOK. CLEARLY DAIJA IS AFRAID OF THIS PERSON.
BUT SHE'S ALSO INVOLVED WITH HIM IN SOME WAY.
THE POINT IS I'M SUPPOSED TO BE THE SUPER HERO. I CAN'T JUST RUN TO HER AND ASK HER TO SOLVE THIS FOR ME.

WELL, YOU KNOW WHAT? SOMETIMES SUPER HEROES MAKE MISTAKES. AND GET HURT.
SUPER HEROES CAN'T FIX EVERYTHING.
SUPER HEROES NEED HELP SOMETIMES.
BEEP BEEP BEEP BEEP
RIRI, THE MOTION SENSORS AROUND THE PERIMETER OF DAIJA'S HOUSE ARE GOING OFF IN A WAY THAT MATCHES HER AMBULATORY SIGNATURES.
AH, THANKS, N.A.T.A.L.I.E.
SO... YOU'RE NOT THINKING ABOUT TRACKING HER...
...YOU ARE TRACKING HER.
SEE, I ONLY HALFWAY LIED TO MY MOM.
I AM TESTING OUT SOME NEW MOTION SENSORS.
I DON'T LIKE ANYTHING ABOUT THIS.
I GET THAT. I REALLY DO.
BUT I STARTED THIS THING, AND I NEED TO FINISH IT.
THANKS AGAIN FOR COMING OVER. I GOTTA GO.
I'LL HOLLER AT YOU LATER.
LET ME KNOW IF...
...YOU NEED ANY HELP.

WHAT IS OUR PLAN, EXACTLY?
NO PLAN. JUST WANNA SEE WHERE SHE'S GOING.
AND WHAT IF SHE SEES YOU?
AH, THERE SHE IS.
SHE WON'T SEE ME. BECAUSE TODAY IS THE PERFECT DAY TO TRY OUT MY NEW...
...STEALTH MODE.
NOT BAD, NOT BAD.
AND ANYWAY, DON'T YOU READ COMICS?
FIRST RULE OF SUPER HEROES: NOBODY EVER LOOKS UP.

— WHAT IS THIS PLACE?!

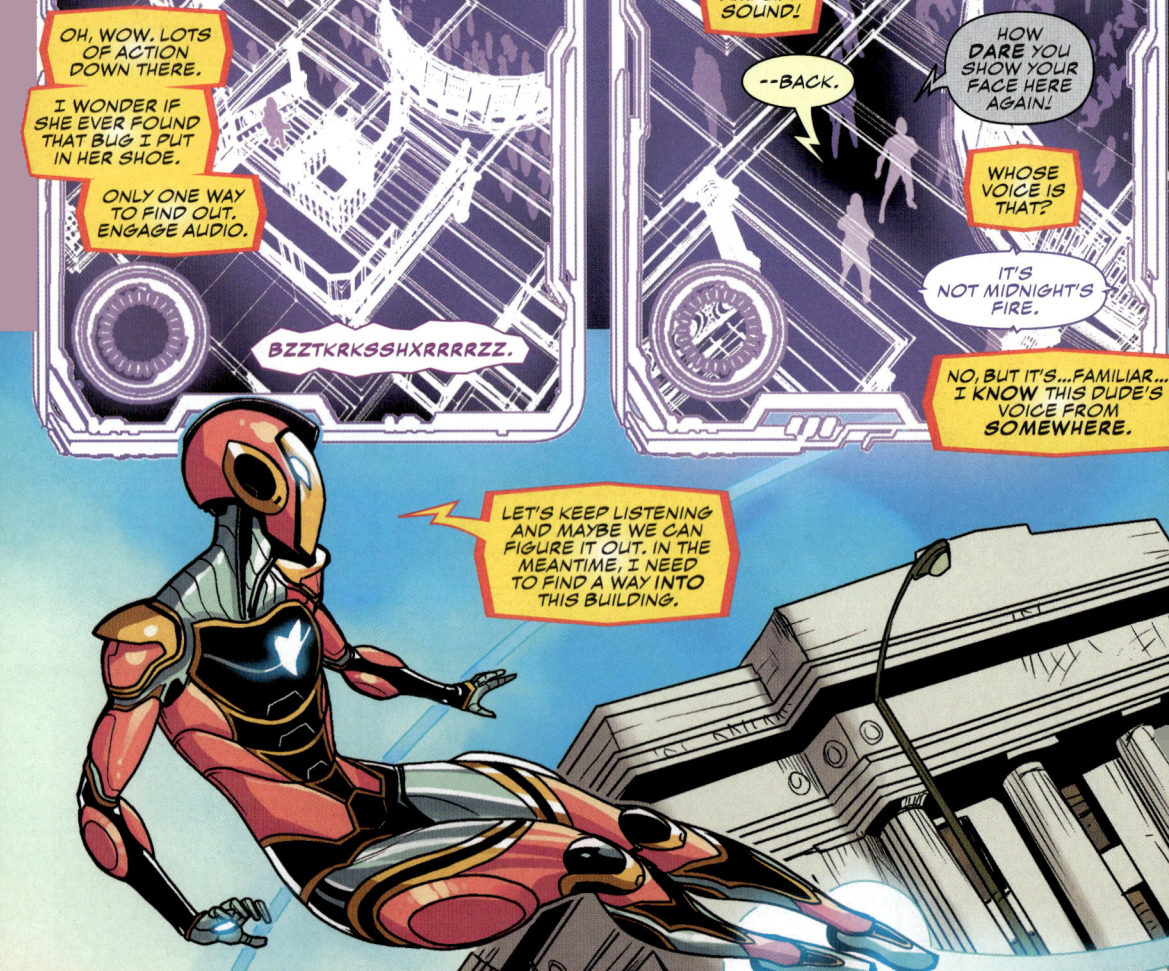

— SHOOT. WE'RE LOSING VISUALS.
— ACTIVATE MEDIUM-RANGE THERMAL IMAGING.

— OH, WOW. LOTS OF ACTION DOWN THERE.
— I WONDER IF SHE EVER FOUND THAT BUG I PUT IN HER SHOE.
— ONLY ONE WAY TO FIND OUT. ENGAGE AUDIO.

BZZTKRKSSHXRRRRZZ.

— AMPLIFY SOUND!
— --BACK.
— HOW DARE YOU SHOW YOUR FACE HERE AGAIN!
— WHOSE VOICE IS THAT?
— IT'S NOT MIDNIGHT'S FIRE.
— NO, BUT IT'S...FAMILIAR. I KNOW THIS DUDE'S VOICE FROM SOMEWHERE.

— LET'S KEEP LISTENING AND MAYBE WE CAN FIGURE IT OUT. IN THE MEANTIME, I NEED TO FIND A WAY INTO THIS BUILDING.

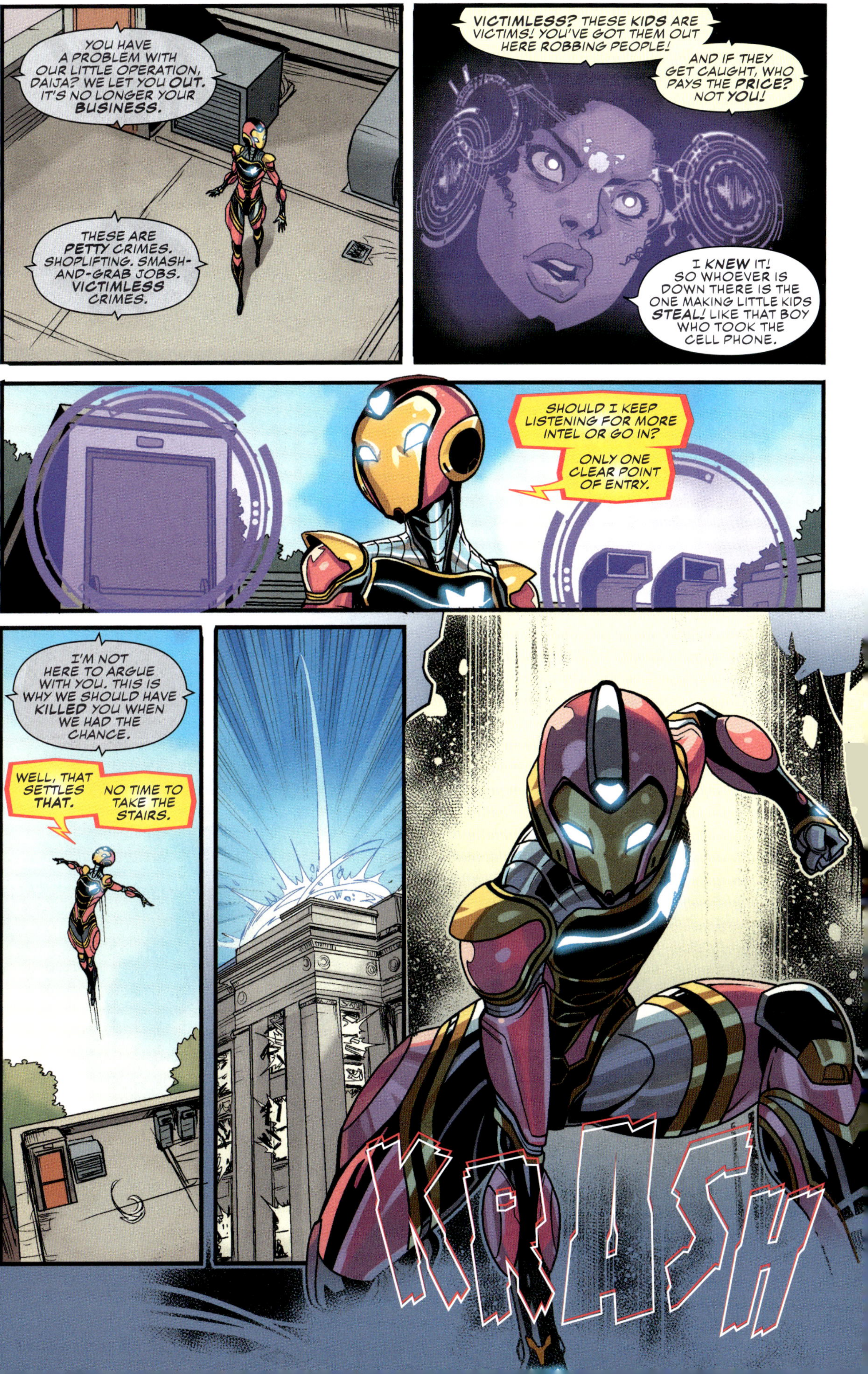

YOU HAVE A PROBLEM WITH OUR LITTLE OPERATION, DAIJA? WE LET YOU OUT. IT'S NO LONGER YOUR BUSINESS.
THESE ARE PETTY CRIMES. SHOPLIFTING. SMASH-AND-GRAB JOBS. VICTIMLESS CRIMES.
VICTIMLESS? THESE KIDS ARE VICTIMS! YOU'VE GOT THEM OUT HERE ROBBING PEOPLE!
AND IF THEY GET CAUGHT, WHO PAYS THE PRICE? NOT YOU!
I KNEW IT! SO WHOEVER IS DOWN THERE IS THE ONE MAKING LITTLE KIDS STEAL! LIKE THAT BOY WHO TOOK THE CELL PHONE.
SHOULD I KEEP LISTENING FOR MORE INTEL OR GO IN?
ONLY ONE CLEAR POINT OF ENTRY.
I'M NOT HERE TO ARGUE WITH YOU. THIS IS WHY WE SHOULD HAVE KILLED YOU WHEN WE HAD THE CHANCE.
WELL, THAT SETTLES THAT.
NO TIME TO TAKE THE STAIRS.
KRASH

WHAT ON EARTH...
DEAR GOD.
DAIJA! WHAT ARE YOU DOING?
ENDING THIS.
THAT VOICE-- IT'S THOMAS BIRCH! THE CITY COUNCIL GUY!
DAIJA! NO!

FREEZE, BOTH OF YOU! DAIJA, DROP IT.
YES! BUT IT'S NOT WORTH IT!
DO YOU SEE WHAT HE'S DONE?!
RIRI!
I'VE GOT THIS! I'VE GOT YOU!
HE USED ME! HE MADE ME THINK THAT HE WANTED GOOD FOR THE CITY!
BUT HE'S JUST USING EVERYONE. USING THESE KIDS. USING PEOPLE'S FEAR.
WHAT DO YOU MEAN, DAIJA?
SHE MEANS I UNDERSTAND WHAT PEOPLE NEED.
HE HAS A DATABASE, RIRI. HE'S STEALING DATA OFF ALL THESE PHONES, THINGS TO HELP HIM WIN HIS GOVERNOR RACE. STEALING SECRETS AND SELLING THEM.
OH, SWEETIE. THIS IS MUCH BIGGER THAN ME. I'M WORKING WITH POWERFUL PEOPLE.
PEOPLE WITH BIG PLANS.
AND YOU'RE USING KIDS?
≥SNORT≤ THESE ARE BARELY KIDS. THEY'RE CRIMINALS. WITH CRIMINAL INSTINCTS. I'M JUST ORGANIZING THEM. PUTTING THEM TO GOOD USE.
AND I'M GIVING PEOPLE WHAT THEY WANT. THEY NEED PANIC, YOU SEE. SOMETHING TO BRING THEM TOGETHER. BRING THEM UNDER CONTROL.
WHAT BETTER THAN A LITTLE CRIME WAVE? NOW THE PEOPLE HAVE A COMMON ENEMY: A BUNCH OF FILTHY THUGS THAT NO ONE CARES ABOUT ANYWAY.

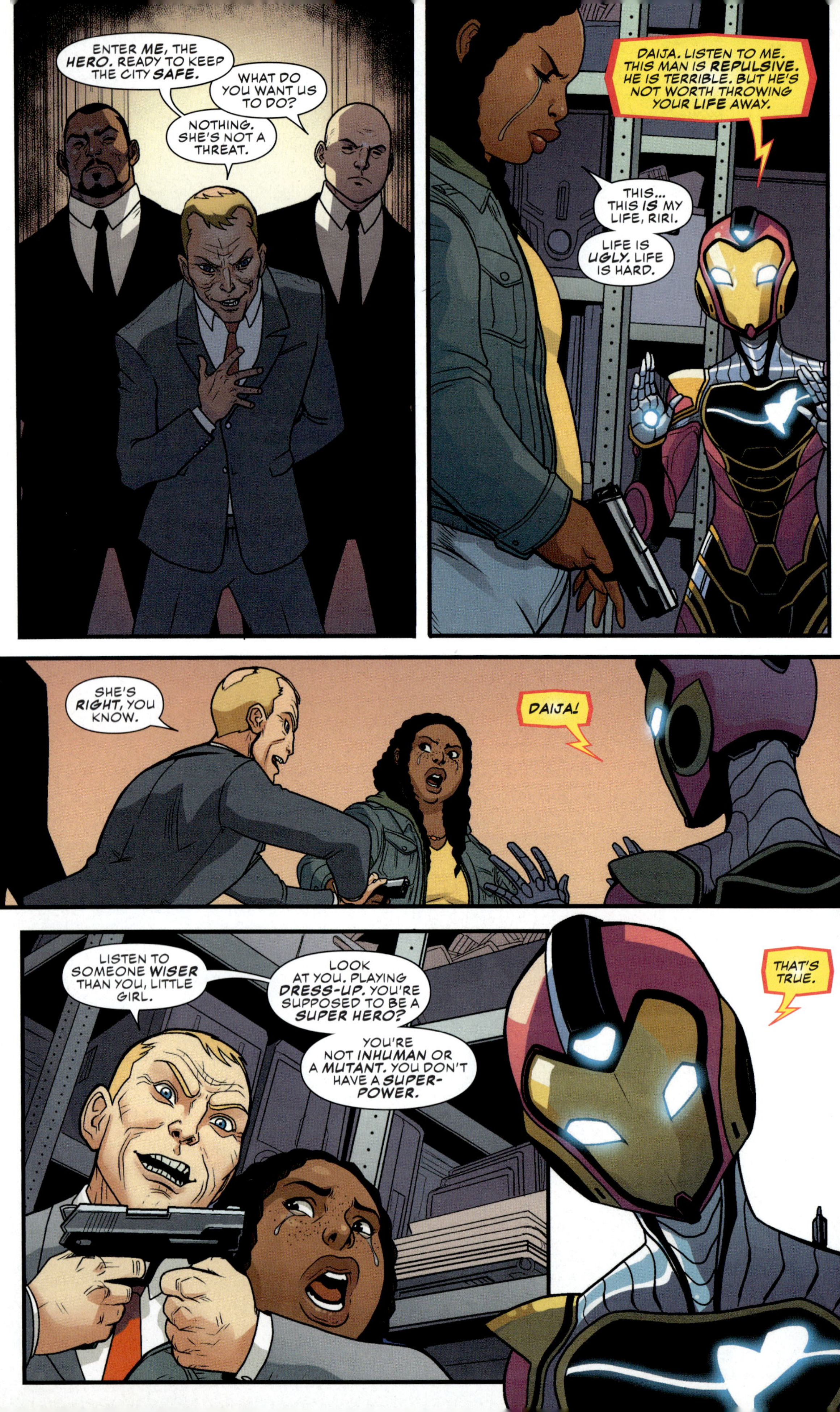
ENTER ME, THE HERO. READY TO KEEP THE CITY SAFE.
WHAT DO YOU WANT US TO DO?
NOTHING. SHE'S NOT A THREAT.
DAIJA. LISTEN TO ME. THIS MAN IS REPULSIVE. HE IS TERRIBLE. BUT HE'S NOT WORTH THROWING YOUR LIFE AWAY.
THIS... THIS IS MY LIFE, RIRI.
LIFE IS UGLY. LIFE IS HARD.
SHE'S RIGHT, YOU KNOW.
DAIJA!
LISTEN TO SOMEONE WISER THAN YOU, LITTLE GIRL.
LOOK AT YOU. PLAYING DRESS-UP. YOU'RE SUPPOSED TO BE A SUPER HERO?
YOU'RE NOT INHUMAN OR A MUTANT. YOU DON'T HAVE A SUPER-POWER.
THAT'S TRUE.

SOMEHOW, I MAKE IT WORK.
UGGGHHH! WHAT IS THAT?
IRON FILINGS SUSPENDED IN A HIGH-VISCOSITY, HIGHLY ADHESIVE LIQUID. HE'S COVERED IN METAL.
AND NOW HE'S A GIANT ELECTRO-MAGNET.
FIGURED I'D MAKE USE OF THIS ENVIRONMENT.
WHAT DO YOU CALL THAT? THE GOO CANNON?
IRON CANNON? IRON SLIME? MAGNET BLAST? I'M SO BAD AT THIS.
YOU REALLY ARE.
LET'S GET--
OH NO.

YOU'VE HAD TOO MANY CHANCES, RIRI WILLIAMS.
DID YOU THINK A FOOL LIKE THIS MAN WOULD BE WORKING ALONE?
HE IS BUT A PAWN. A TOOL IN THE SERVICE OF DESTINY.
THE DESTINY YOU FOOLISHLY REJECTED.
DAIJA, GET THE KIDS!
I NEED TO FIND A WAY FOR THEM TO GET OUT!
THERE! SEWER TUNNEL! WATCH OUT, I'M GONNA BLOW OPEN THAT WALL!
RUN!
LET'S GO, Y'ALL! MOVE!

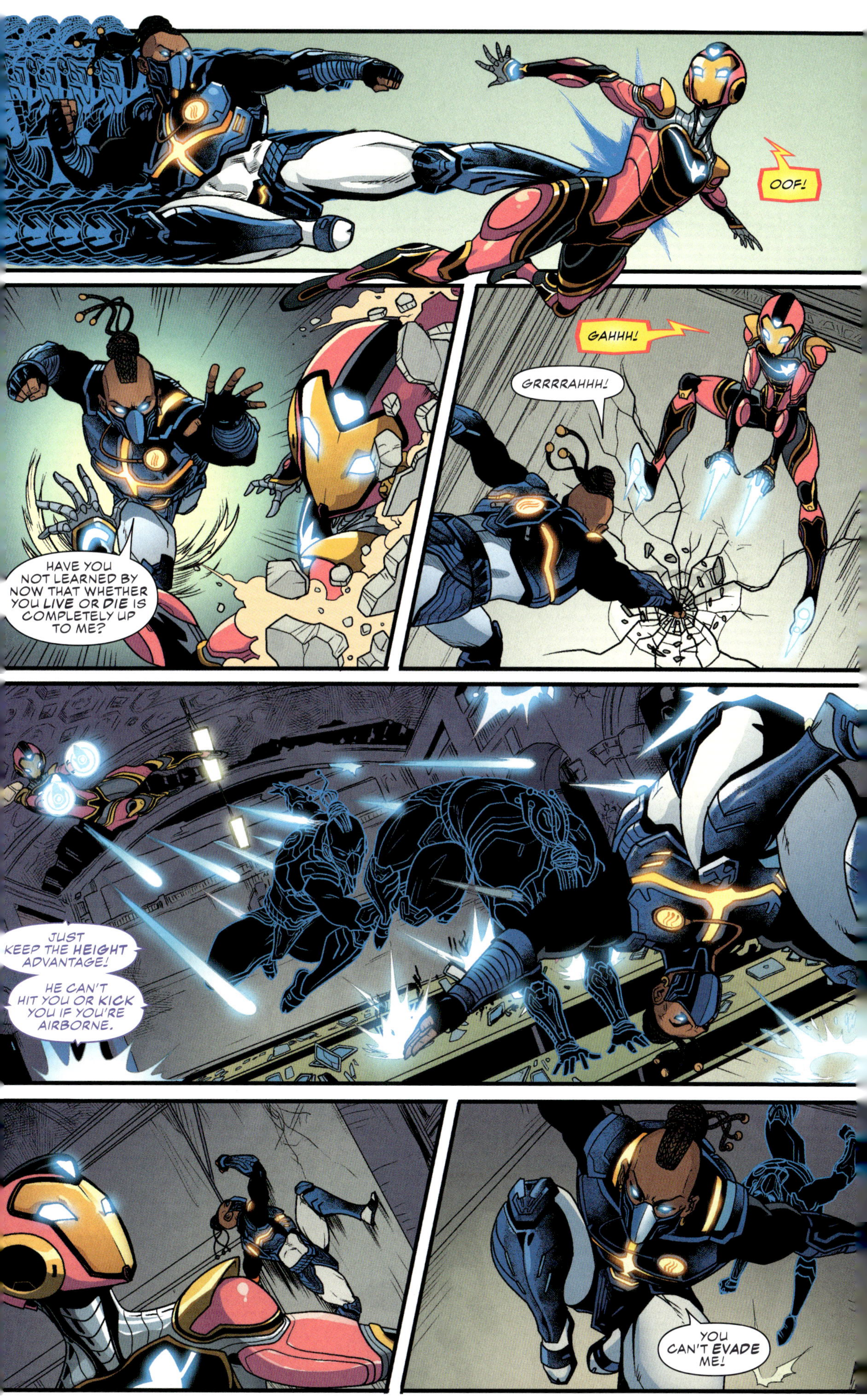
OOF!
HAVE YOU NOT LEARNED BY NOW THAT WHETHER YOU LIVE OR DIE IS COMPLETELY UP TO ME?
GAHHH!
GRRRRAHHH!
JUST KEEP THE HEIGHT ADVANTAGE!
HE CAN'T HIT YOU OR KICK YOU IF YOU'RE AIRBORNE.
YOU CAN'T EVADE ME!

GET--
KRRZAP
--OFF ME!
HE'S KNOCKED OUT. LET'S GO!
WE CAN'T. HE COULD WAKE UP ANYTIME, AND DAIJA AND THE KIDS ARE RIGHT OUTSIDE.
IT'S TOO DANGEROUS.
OOF.
POLICE!

DON'T SHOOT!
WE HAVE REPORTS OF SHOTS FIRED AT THIS LOCATION.
AND THIS IS A LOT OF STOLEN MERCHANDISE YOU GOT HERE.
HELLO, OFFICERS. I CAN EXPLAIN. THIS WAS--
DON'T SAY BIRCH! YOU HAVE NO IDEA WHO HE HAS IN HIS POCKET!
THIS WAS--A SUPER VILLAIN.
MATTER OF FACT, HE'S RIGHT INSIDE THAT VAULT.
SUPER VILLAIN, HUH?
HIS NAME IS MIDNIGHT'S FIRE. HE--
--IS GONE.
THAT'S IT. YOU'RE UNDER ARREST.
WAIT! I HAVE VIDEO PROOF!
SEE? HE WAS HERE.
HUH. OKAY.
SHOULD WE WRITE THIS UP?
NUTCASE WHO WALKS THROUGH WALLS? THAT'S A LOT OF PAPERWORK.

YES, MA'AM. I HAVE HIM RIGHT HERE. NEAR 115TH AND MORGAN.
OKAY, WE'LL BE WAITING.
SO NO ONE CAN COME GET YOU?
MY MAMA DON'T GET OFF 'TIL 3.
IT'S WAY AFTER 3.
NO, 3 A.M.
OH... OH.
MY DADDY HAS TO STAY IN LINE AT THE SHELTER OR WE WON'T GET A SPOT.
OUR PHONE IS CUT OFF.
OURS TOO.
OKAY.
WE'LL GET EVERYONE HOME.
HOW?
I DECIDED TO CALL A FRIEND.
BEEP, BEEP! I'VE GOT ROOM FOR FOUR PEOPLE.
THE HORN ON THIS CAR DOESN'T ACTUALLY WORK.
HA, OKAY! BUT...IT'S SIX OF US.
IT'S HANDLED.
I'LL... BE SEEING YOU.

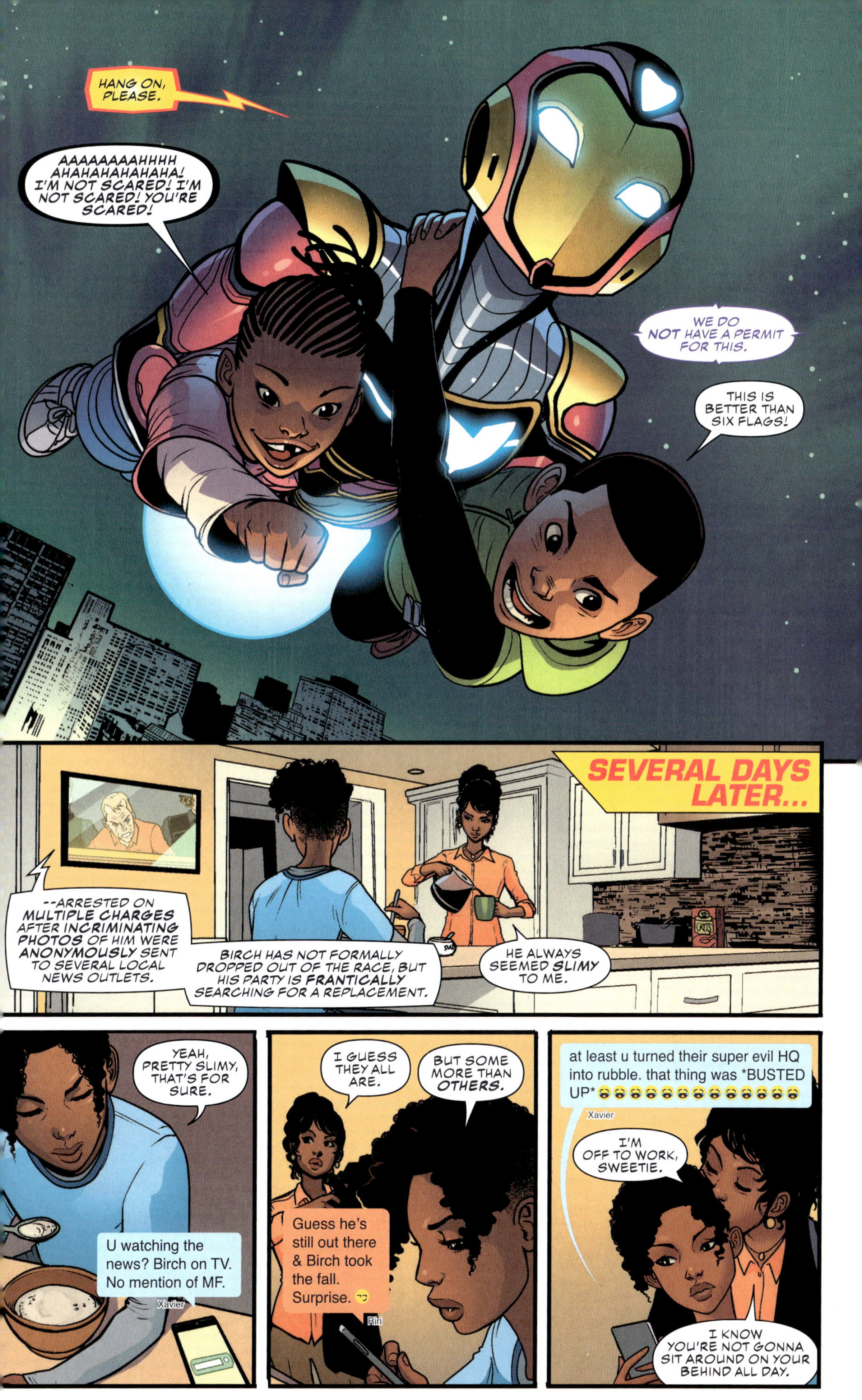
HANG ON, PLEASE.
AAAAAAAAHHHH AHAHAHAHAHAHA! I'M NOT SCARED! I'M NOT SCARED! YOU'RE SCARED!
WE DO NOT HAVE A PERMIT FOR THIS.
THIS IS BETTER THAN SIX FLAGS!
SEVERAL DAYS LATER...
--ARRESTED ON MULTIPLE CHARGES AFTER INCRIMINATING PHOTOS OF HIM WERE ANONYMOUSLY SENT TO SEVERAL LOCAL NEWS OUTLETS.
BIRCH HAS NOT FORMALLY DROPPED OUT OF THE RACE, BUT HIS PARTY IS FRANTICALLY SEARCHING FOR A REPLACEMENT.
HE ALWAYS SEEMED SLIMY TO ME.
YEAH, PRETTY SLIMY, THAT'S FOR SURE.
U watching the news? Birch on TV. No mention of MF.
Xavier
I GUESS THEY ALL ARE.
BUT SOME MORE THAN OTHERS.
Guess he's still out there & Birch took the fall. Surprise.
Riri
at least u turned their super evil HQ into rubble. that thing was *BUSTED UP*
Xavier
I'M OFF TO WORK, SWEETIE.
I KNOW YOU'RE NOT GONNA SIT AROUND ON YOUR BEHIND ALL DAY.

ACTUALLY, MOTHER DEAREST, I'M GOING INTO THE LAB TODAY.
THE LAB? WELL, I KNOW I SAID I WANTED YOU TO GO BACK TO SCHOOL. BUT... YOU'RE FLYING ALL THE WAY BACK TO CAMBRIDGE TODAY? ON A SATURDAY?
MMM, NOT THE M.I.T. LAB.
I'M GOING TO THE NEW LAB.
WHAT NEW LAB? WHERE'D YOU GET MONEY FOR THAT?
TURNS OUT, IMPORTANT PEOPLE GET REALLY GENEROUS WHEN YOU FILL THEM IN ABOUT THEIR STOLEN ELECTRONICS AND BREACHES OF THEIR SENSITIVE DATA.
WHICH REMINDS ME. I LEFT A LITTLE BIT OF BILL MONEY ON YOUR DRESSER.
OH, HONEY. I DON'T NEED YOU TO--
LET ME DO THIS ONE THING, MOM.
AND IT LOOKS LIKE I'M GONNA BEAT YOU TO WORK. HAVE A GOOD DAY, MOMMY. LOVE YOU.
OHANDALSO
I SOLD A PATENT FOR A TINY AUDIO RECORDER WITH A BUILT-IN GPS TRACKER THAT FITS ON A SHOE.
OKAY I'LL BE HOME FOR DINNER BYYYYYEEEEEEE!
SO YOU'RE NOT GOING BACK TO--YOU KNOW WHAT?
WE'LL TALK ABOUT THIS LATER, RIRI!
THESE KIDS. SHE BECOMES A SUPER HERO AND SUDDENLY I'M BOOBOO THE FOOL. WELL, I'LL TELL YOU ONE THING--
--YOU BETTER WASH THESE DISHES UP WHEN YOU GET BACK!

LATER THAT DAY.
SOMEWHERE IN CHICAGO...
OKAY. LET'S REVIEW. RULE NUMBER ONE: THIS LOCATION IS SECRET.
CAN EVERYONE HERE KEEP IT A SECRET?
UH, WE KEPT THE OTHER UNDERGROUND LAIR A SECRET.
AND THAT ONE DIDN'T HAVE FRUIT SNACKS.
WE GOOD.
GOOD. RULE TWO: YOU CAN COME HERE EVERY ONCE IN A WHILE IF YOU NEED A SAFE PLACE.
BUT NO SKIPPING SCHOOL.
ANY QUESTIONS?
YES?
I HAVE A PEANUT ALLERGY!
OKAY. RULE NUMBER THREE: NO PEANUTS.

IT AIN'T EXACTLY THE TRISKELION.
RIRIIIIIIIII! MARCUS PUT A MAGNET IN HIS MOUTH!
STOP SNITCHING!
YOU'RE RIGHT.
BUT EVERYONE HAS TO START SOMEWHERE.
LITTLE BOY! YES, YOU, WITH THE BIG HEAD! SPIT THAT OUT!
AN HOUR LATER...
RI.
5:30.
HM.
...
YOU PROMISED YOUR MOM.
OKAYYYYYY.
CAN YOU--
YOU'RE SUCH A BABY.
I'LL MAKE SURE THE KIDS GET HOME. AND I'LL LOCK UP.
THANKS, N.A.T.A.L.I.E.
FOR REAL.
NOT TOO FAR AWAY...
CHICAGO BAPTIST CHURCH
MEETING TONIGHT
HI, EVERYONE. I'VE MET SOME OF YOU BEFORE. MY NAME IS RONNIE, AND I'M...

...I'M HERE WITH MY DAUGHTER, RIRI.

WE LOST MY HUSBAND, WHICH YOU ALREADY KNOW ABOUT. BUT RIRI ALSO LOST HER BEST FRIEND THAT DAY.

HONEY, DO YOU WANT TO INTRODUCE YOURSELF?

UM. HI.

TONIGHT
FAMILY
GUN VIOLENCE
SUPPORT GROUP

MY NAME IS RIRI WILLIAMS.

AND I'M...STILL WORKING ON SOME THINGS.

6

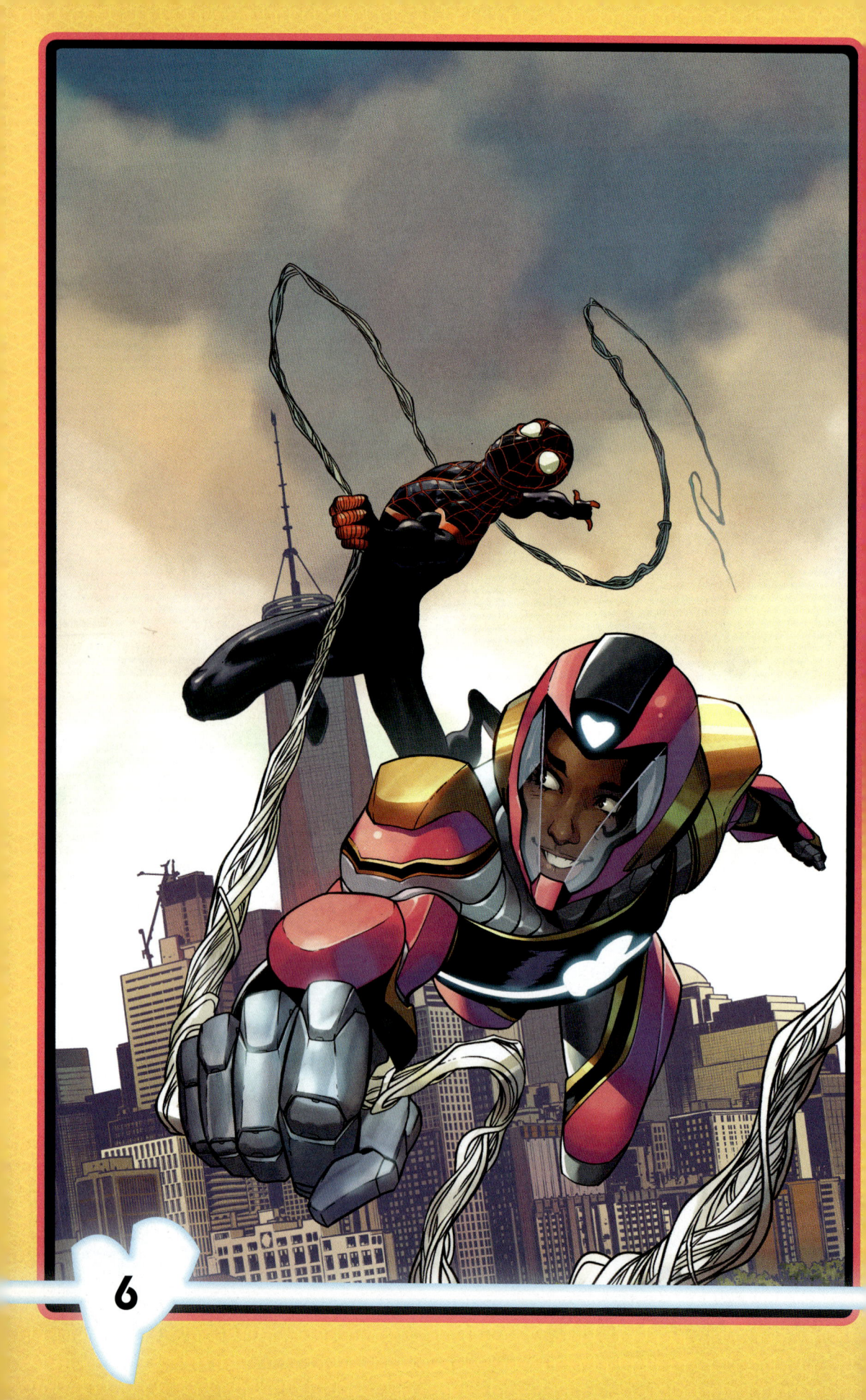

I'VE NEVER BEEN *GREAT* AT THE WHOLE "FRIENDSHIP" THING.

I'M WORKING ON IT. I REALLY AM.

BUT THE TROUBLE IS, ONCE YOU START CARING ABOUT PEOPLE...

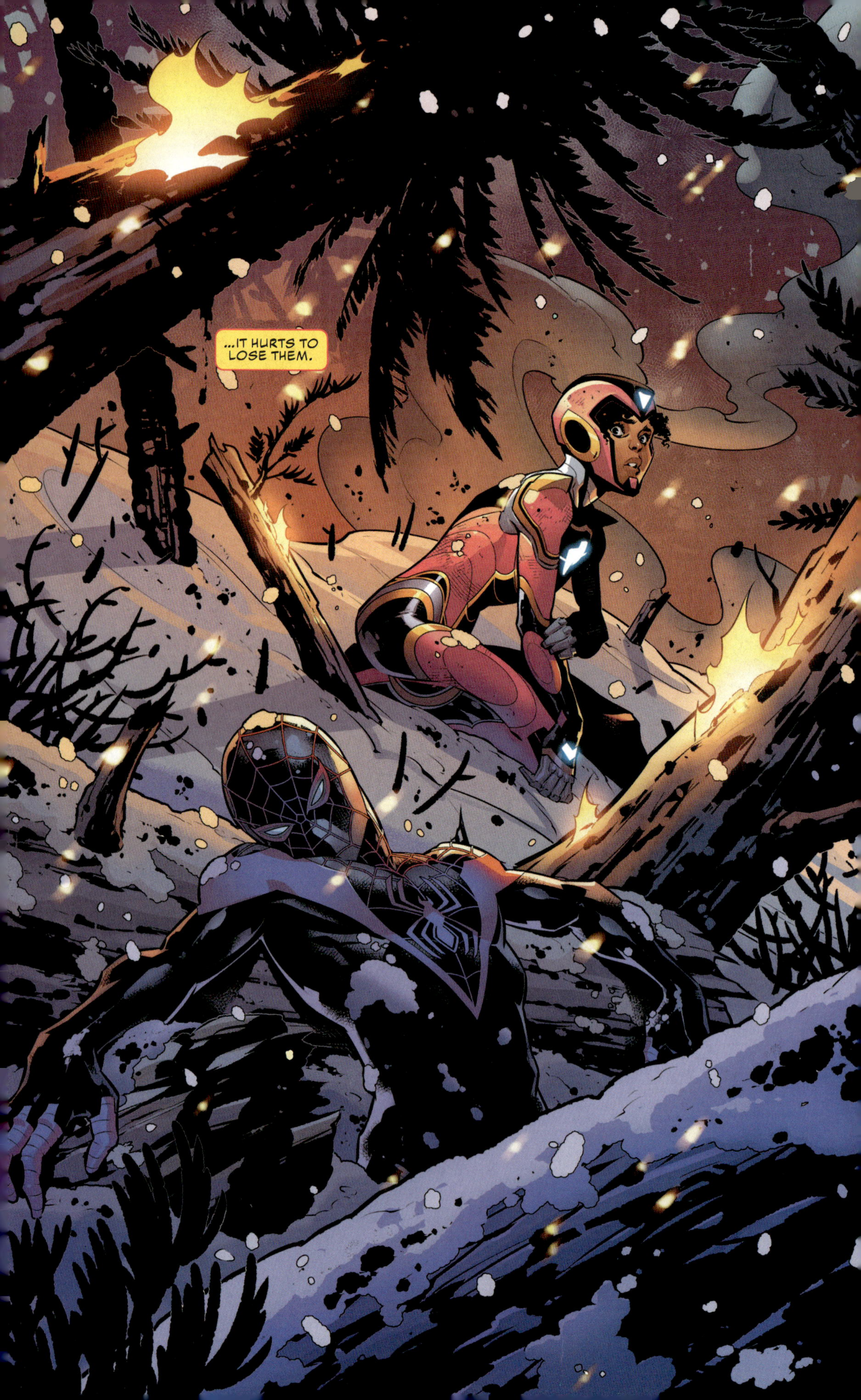
...IT HURTS TO LOSE THEM.

CHICAGO. ONE DAY EARLIER.

I CHECKED THE POLICE RECORDS. HIS PARENTS FILED A MISSING PERSONS REPORT, BUT NO LEADS. I'M GONNA HEAD OUT TOMORROW.

I DON'T WANT YOU TO GO ALONE. THIS SHOULD BE A CHAMPIONS MISSION.

YOU'RE THE ONE WHO SAID MILES DOESN'T LIKE TO BE SMOTHERED, MS. MARVEL.

I GUESS YOU'RE RIGHT. AFTER WHAT HAPPENED* HE WON'T RESPOND TO SOMEONE FAWNING OVER HIM, ACTING ALL WARM AND FUZZY.

SO YOU'RE PERFECT FOR THIS MISSION.

SHE'S RIGHT, THOUGH. I THOUGHT YOU AND MILES DON'T REALLY GET ALONG.

WHY ARE WE DOING THIS AGAIN?

BECAUSE.

*SEE CHAMPIONS #4. --E.E.

THANKS.

SORRY.

A FEW MONTHS AGO.

"I think... I think I've just been feeling out of place."

"If you quit this team, I will kick your butt."

"I'm not going anywhere."

"Okay, good."

"He made me a promise."

"And besides. We all need somebody to come after us sometimes."

"Facts."

"We haven't heard from him in a couple weeks. He could be in danger."

"I'll keep you updated, fearless leader. Promise. Okay?"

"Okay. Later."

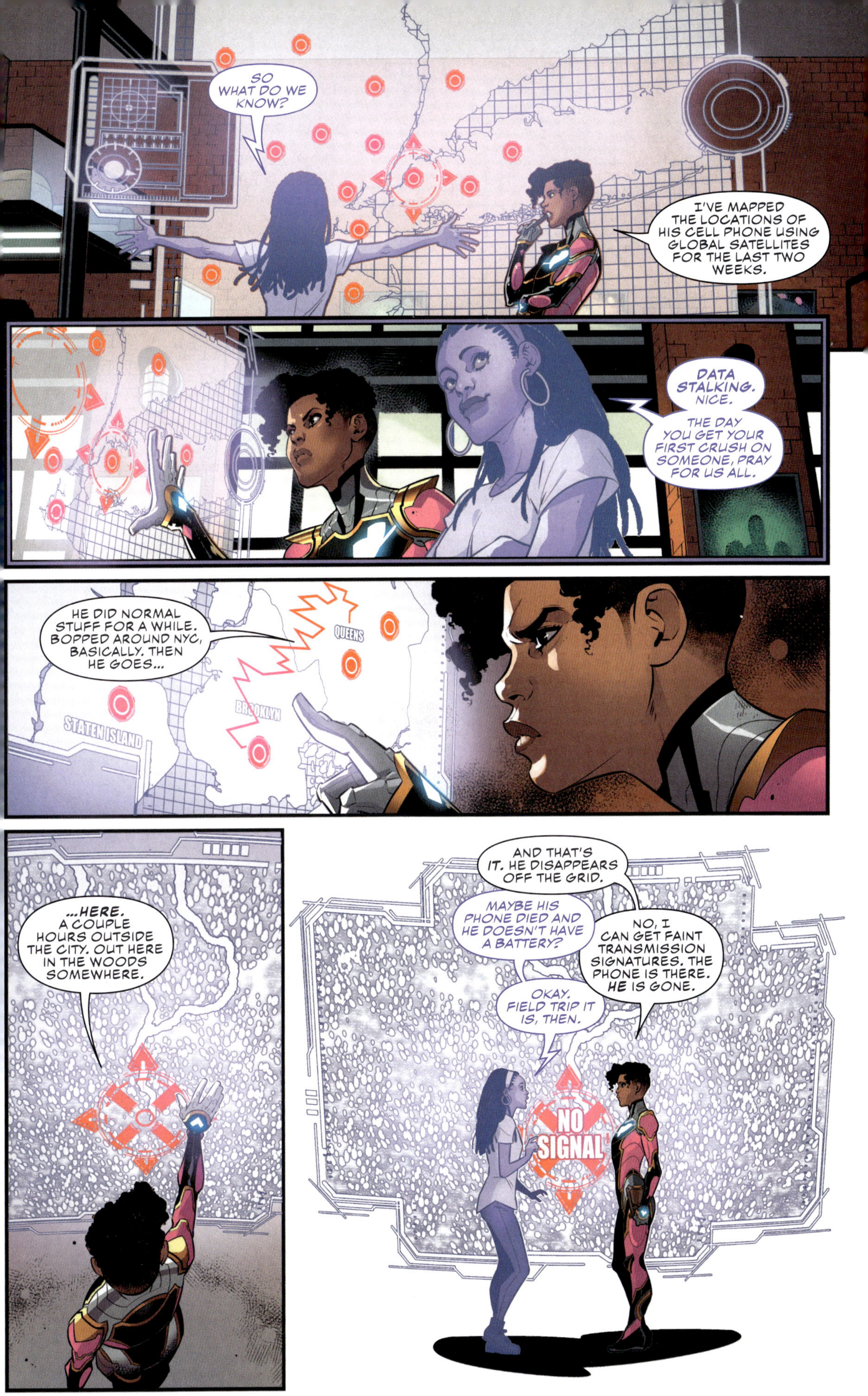
SO WHAT DO WE KNOW?
I'VE MAPPED THE LOCATIONS OF HIS CELL PHONE USING GLOBAL SATELLITES FOR THE LAST TWO WEEKS.
DATA STALKING. NICE.
THE DAY YOU GET YOUR FIRST CRUSH ON SOMEONE, PRAY FOR US ALL.
HE DID NORMAL STUFF FOR A WHILE. BOPPED AROUND NYC, BASICALLY. THEN HE GOES...
QUEENS
BROOKLYN
STATEN ISLAND
...HERE. A COUPLE HOURS OUTSIDE THE CITY. OUT HERE IN THE WOODS SOMEWHERE.
AND THAT'S IT. HE DISAPPEARS OFF THE GRID.
MAYBE HIS PHONE DIED AND HE DOESN'T HAVE A BATTERY?
NO, I CAN GET FAINT TRANSMISSION SIGNATURES. THE PHONE IS THERE. HE IS GONE.
OKAY. FIELD TRIP IT IS, THEN.
NO SIGNAL

UPSTATE NEW YORK.
THE NEXT DAY.
I DON'T THINK WE'RE IN CHICAGO ANYMORE.
THAT CABIN MATCHES THE COORDINATES OF MILES' LAST REGISTERED LOCATION.
I GUESS THE TREES COVERED IT FROM SATELLITE VIEW.
DAY 16. UNKNOWN (HUMAN? CYBORG?) PARTY ARRIVES AT SUBJECT TEST SITE.
OF ALL THE PLACES TO DISAPPEAR? REALLY, MILES? A REMOTE CABIN IN A FOREST?
THIS GOES AGAINST EVERYTHING I HAVE BEEN TAUGHT TO DO BY EVERY HORROR MOVIE EVER.
TALK ABOUT TAKING ONE FOR THE TEAM.
A WITCH PROBABLY LIVES HERE.
KNOCK KNOCK
HELLO?
MILES? MI--
whoosh

WHAT JUST HAPPENED?!
WHAT THE--
MILES?!
YES? HI? AM I UNDER ARREST?
WHAT ARE YOU DOING HERE?!
MAKING... PANCAKES? WHAT ARE YOU DOING HERE?
YOU'VE BEEN MAKING PANCAKES FOR TWO WEEKS?! AND COULDN'T RESPOND TO ANYBODY WONDERING WHERE YOU WERE?
YOU'RE BEING A LITTLE DRAMATIC, DON'T YOU THINK? I'VE BEEN GONE FOR ALL OF A DAY. AND I HAVE A RIGHT TO GET SOME ALONE TIME.
I DON'T NEED YOU HERE TELLING ME EVERYTHING YOU DON'T LIKE ABOUT ME.
I'M NOT BEING DRAMATIC. YOU'VE BEEN GONE FOR SIXTEEN DAYS. TODAY IS--
TICK
TICK
TICK

WHY DOES MY WATCH SAY JANUARY 18TH?!
MY GUESS WOULD BE... BECAUSE IT'S JANUARY 18TH?
SO IF WE'RE AGREED ON THAT, FEEL FREE TO SEE YOURSELF OUT. THIS IS MY FRIEND'S FAMILY CABIN AND I FEEL WEIRD ABOUT HAVING GUESTS.
MILES. IT'S FEBRUARY 2ND. YOU'VE BEEN GONE FOR OVER TWO WEEKS.
I...I CAME TO LOOK FOR YOU.
I TALKED TO XAVIER... YESTERDAY... ABOUT A VALENTINE'S DANCE AT HIS SCHOOL.
HE SAID, "I ONLY HAVE TWO WEEKS TO FIND AN OUTFIT." IT'S FEBRUARY.
JANUARY
RIRI... ARE YOU OKAY?
YOUR PHONE. THE SIGNAL WAS--
JANUARY AGAIN. WHAT IS GOING ON HERE?
JANUARY 18
SOMEONE IS DOING THIS. I'M GONNA GO AND SEE--
whoosh

RIRI? WHAT ARE YOU DOING HERE?
WHA-- WHAT? HOW?
WHERE ARE WE?
THIS PLACE BELONGS TO A RICH KID IN MY CLASS.
HIS FAMILY COMES HERE ON VACATION AND HE OFFERED TO LET ME CHILL HERE FOR A WHILE.
I FELT LIKE I NEEDED A FEW DAYS AWAY AFTER... EVERYTHING...WENT DOWN. TOOK A BUS UP HERE.
WHAT DAY IS IT?
LET'S SEE...IT'S JANUARY 18TH.
N.A.T.A.L.I.E., HOW MANY MINUTES HAVE ELAPSED SINCE OUR LANDING OUTSIDE?
THAT WOULD BE...CARRY THE ONE...
ZERO MINUTES.
RIRI. WHAT'S GOING ON? TELL ME WHY YOU'RE HERE.
THIS HAPPENED ALREADY. I CAME IN, YOU HAD THE SPOON--
WHAT?!
IT ALL HAPPENED ALREADY!

I'M GONNA NEED YOU TO EXPLAIN.
AND ALSO, TO NOT PUT YOUR SUIT THAT'S BEEN ALL OUTSIDE ON THIS EXPENSIVE COUCH.
OKAY. YOU KNOW HOW SOMETIMES WEIRD SUPER HERO STUFF HAPPENS AND IT SOUNDS NUTS BUT YOU JUST HAVE TO BELIEVE IT?
YES.
YOU'VE BEEN MISSING FOR A LONG TIME. EVERYONE IS WORRIED. I LEFT YESTERDAY, WHICH WAS ABSOLUTELY, ONE HUNDRED PERCENT FEBRUARY 1ST, ON A MISSION TO FIND YOU. I TRACKED YOU HERE.
YOU TOLD ME IT WAS JANUARY 18TH AND THAT YOU'D ONLY BEEN HERE FOR A DAY. I FREAKED OUT AND LEFT. I HEARD A SOUND LIKE AN INTENSE WIND AND I BLINKED AND I WAS BACK IN HERE AGAIN.
AND I ASSURE YOU MY ARMOR IS IMPECCABLY CLEAN.
OKAY, YEAH, THAT DOES SOUND NUTS.
BUT I BELIEVE YOU!

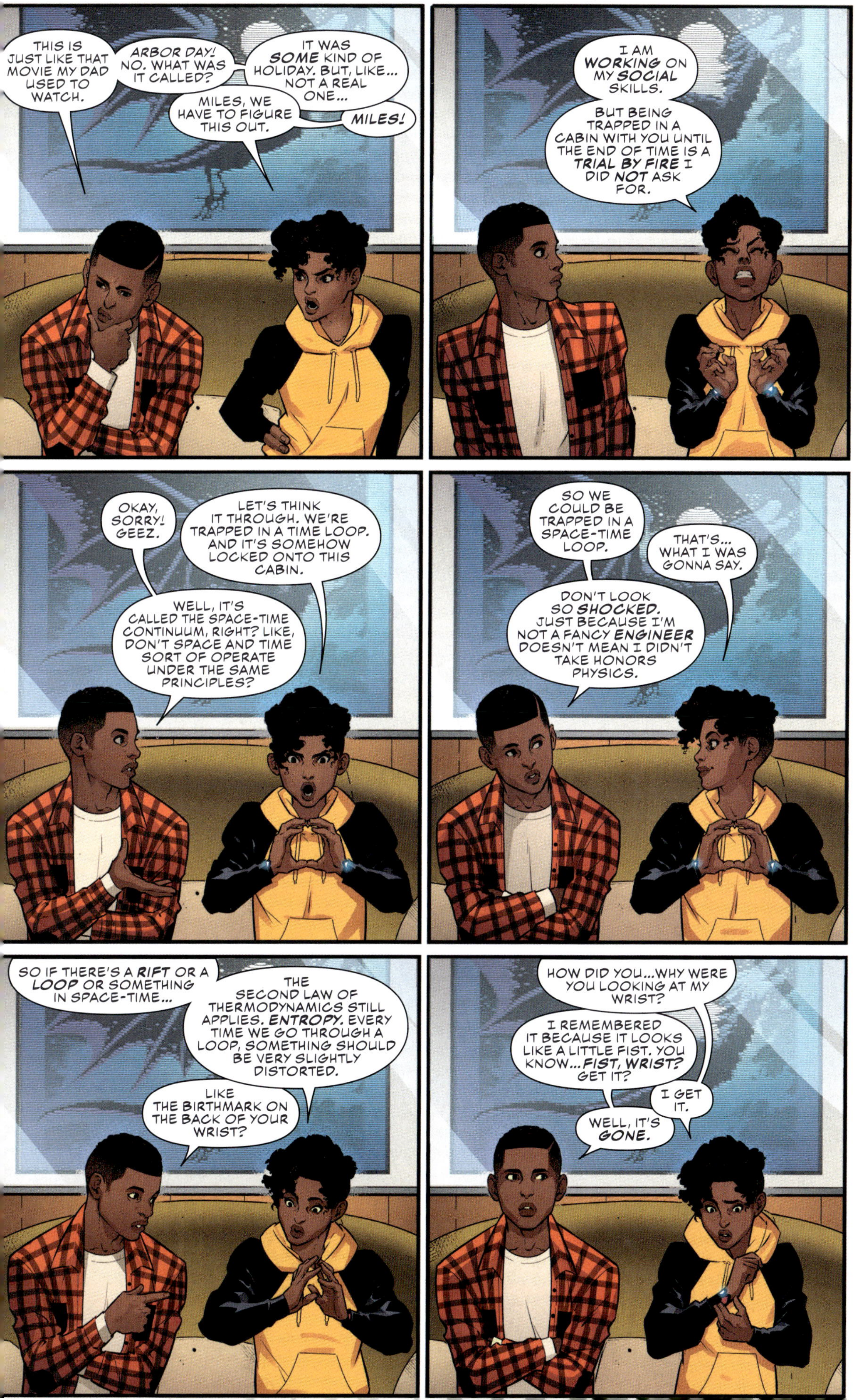

THIS IS JUST LIKE THAT MOVIE MY DAD USED TO WATCH.
ARBOR DAY! NO. WHAT WAS IT CALLED?
IT WAS SOME KIND OF HOLIDAY. BUT, LIKE... NOT A REAL ONE...
MILES, WE HAVE TO FIGURE THIS OUT.
MILES!
I AM WORKING ON MY SOCIAL SKILLS.
BUT BEING TRAPPED IN A CABIN WITH YOU UNTIL THE END OF TIME IS A TRIAL BY FIRE I DID NOT ASK FOR.
OKAY, SORRY! GEEZ.
LET'S THINK IT THROUGH. WE'RE TRAPPED IN A TIME LOOP. AND IT'S SOMEHOW LOCKED ONTO THIS CABIN.
WELL, IT'S CALLED THE SPACE-TIME CONTINUUM, RIGHT? LIKE, DON'T SPACE AND TIME SORT OF OPERATE UNDER THE SAME PRINCIPLES?
SO WE COULD BE TRAPPED IN A SPACE-TIME LOOP.
THAT'S... WHAT I WAS GONNA SAY.
DON'T LOOK SO SHOCKED. JUST BECAUSE I'M NOT A FANCY ENGINEER DOESN'T MEAN I DIDN'T TAKE HONORS PHYSICS.
SO IF THERE'S A RIFT OR A LOOP OR SOMETHING IN SPACE-TIME...
THE SECOND LAW OF THERMODYNAMICS STILL APPLIES. ENTROPY. EVERY TIME WE GO THROUGH A LOOP, SOMETHING SHOULD BE VERY SLIGHTLY DISTORTED.
LIKE THE BIRTHMARK ON THE BACK OF YOUR WRIST?
HOW DID YOU...WHY WERE YOU LOOKING AT MY WRIST?
I REMEMBERED IT BECAUSE IT LOOKS LIKE A LITTLE FIST. YOU KNOW...FIST, WRIST? GET IT?
I GET IT.
WELL, IT'S GONE.

BUT THERE'S STILL THE PREDESTINATION PARADOX.
THE WHAT?
DON'T YOU WATCH STAR TREK?
WE HAVEN'T BEEN IN THE LOOP FOREVER, RIGHT? WE HAVE MEMORIES FROM BEFORE. SO SOMEONE HAD TO START THE LOOP.
YOU SHOULD SUIT UP.
STAR TREK IS NOT REAL SCIENCE!
REAL SCIENCE--?! OKAY, LOOK WHO'S TALKING, GUY-WHO-TURNS-INVISIBLE!
POINT TAKEN.
SOMEONE CAUSED THIS.
AND FOR IT TO KEEP GOING INSTEAD OF JUST LOOPING ONCE, THEY HAVE TO BE CONSISTENTLY DOING IT.
WHICH MEANS THEY'RE EITHER A GOD...OR THEY'RE NEARBY.
DOES THIS HOUSE HAVE INSURANCE?
PROBABLY.
GOOD.
WHY DID WE SUIT UP? ARE WE GOING OUT--

OH.
N.A.T.A.L.I.E., WHAT DAY IS IT?
FEBRUARY 2ND.
JUST AS I THOUGHT. THE DOOR WAS THE VESSEL FOR THE RIFT.
COULDN'T WE HAVE JUST GONE OUT THE WINDOW?
IT'S NOT THAT BAD.
YOU REALLY DON'T HAVE ANY SOCIAL SKILLS. WHO IS GONNA PAY FOR THIS?!
INSURANCE!
THAT'S NOT HOW INSURANCE WORKS!
WELL, NOW YOU'VE GONE AND RUINED MY EXPERIMENT.

"I was going for *thirty days* of logged observation. And you've messed that all up."

"Who's there?!"

"The tank."

"You don't know me. But I know *you*. I've been watching you. *Testing* you."

"I've got something of an unorthodox interest in space, time, interdimensional portals, *that* sort of thing."

"I'm a *hobbyist*, really. A connoisseur."

"Watching me?"

MILES, THIS GUY IS A STRING BEAN. A DELUSIONAL STRING BEAN.
I DON'T KNOW. THERE'S... SOMETHING MORE TO HIM. HE'S THROWING ME OFF.
YOU WOULD BE WISE TO TRUST YOUR FRIEND'S INSTINCTS.
WHY WERE YOU WATCHING ME?! WHAT DO YOU WANT?
NOTHING PERSONAL. AS I SAID, AN EXPERIMENT. I'M INTERESTED IN S.S.S.T.P.s.
THE YOUNG MAN EMITS THE FAINT QUANTUM SIGNATURES TYPICAL OF INTERDIMENSIONAL TRAVELERS. SO I TRACKED HIM HERE.
S.S.S.T.P.s?
SMALL-SCALE SPACE-TIME PORTALS.
OH. THAT ACTUALLY SOUNDS LIKE IT COULD BE REALLY INTERESTING.
LISTEN, THOUGH, CREEPY STALKER GUY. YOU'RE--
NOO!

YOU'VE DESTROYED MY STUDY! ALL MY EFFORT, RUINED.
WHAT IS HE?!
LOOKS LIKE SOME KIND OF MUTANT WITH METAMORPHIC POWERS.
WE CAN TAKE HIM! WE--
AHHH!
NOW...
...YOU BURN.

KAFF KAFF
MILES!
MILES! ARE YOU CONSCIOUS?
HIS VITALS ARE STABLE.
I'M... I'M OKAY. I'M UP.
GOOD. ENOUGH OF THIS GUY.
BRACE YOURSELF.
LET'S GO.
GRAAAAWR!
THWIP
THWIP
DON'T THINK SO.

WE GOT HIM ON THE ROPES!
RIRI, LOOK OUT!
A PORTAL!
MOVE!
PULL HIM IN!
GOTCHA!
VREEEM

WHAT HAPPENS NOW?
HE'LL CYCLE THROUGH THE PORTALS LIKE THAT INFINITELY, GRADUALLY FACING SUB-ATOMIC ATTRITION UNTIL HE CEASES TO EXIST.
OR I CAN SEND A DISTRESS SIGNAL TO THE FOREST SERVICE.
LET'S GO WITH THAT ONE.
RIRI...I JUST...I JUST WANNA KNOW WHY.
WHY'D I BLAST THE DOOR? I FIGURED ANYONE WITH "VACATION HOUSE" MONEY HAS "BUY A NEW DOOR" MONEY.
NOT THAT.
WHY DID YOU COME UP HERE?
OH.
IT JUST ALWAYS SEEMED LIKE YOU DIDN'T LIKE ME.
I DON'T LIKE MOST PEOPLE. BUT YOU...YOU'RE MY TEAMMATE. TEAMMATES CHECK ON EACH OTHER.
FRIENDS CHECK ON EACH OTHER.
ARE WE...ARE WE FRIENDS?
WELL, WHEN I ESCAPED FROM A FLAMING PILE OF TREES TO SAVE YOU, THAT'S THE ASSUMPTION I WAS WORKING WITH!
HEY! I HAVE SUPER-STRENGTH. I WOULD HAVE GOTTEN OUT.
...THANKS, THOUGH.

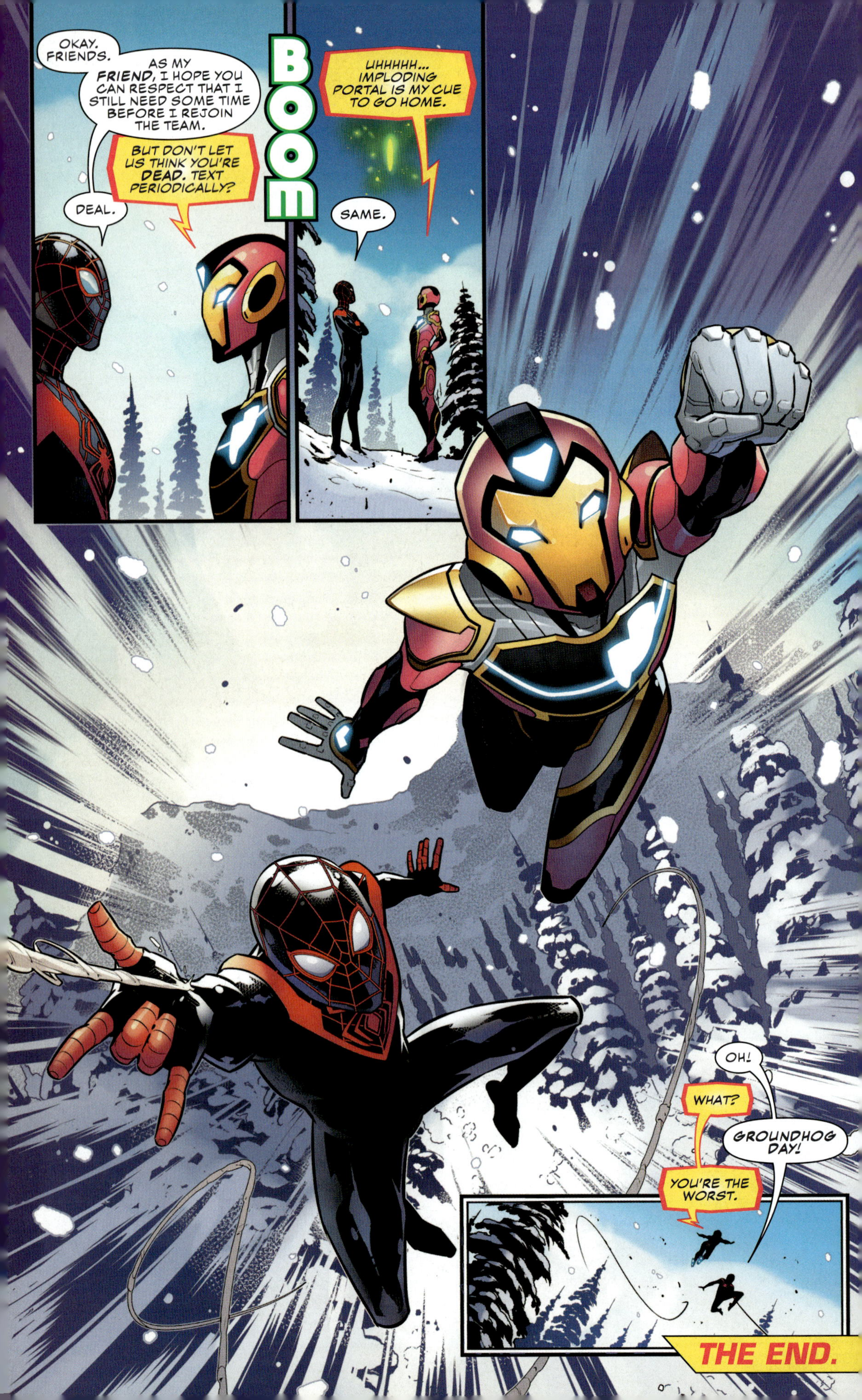
OKAY. FRIENDS.
AS MY FRIEND, I HOPE YOU CAN RESPECT THAT I STILL NEED SOME TIME BEFORE I REJOIN THE TEAM.
BUT DON'T LET US THINK YOU'RE DEAD. TEXT PERIODICALLY?
DEAL.
BOOM
UHHHHH... IMPLODING PORTAL IS MY CUE TO GO HOME.
SAME.
OH!
WHAT?
GROUNDHOG DAY!
YOU'RE THE WORST.
THE END.

LUCIANO VECCHIO
#1 VARIANT

HUMBERTO RAMOS & EDGAR DELGADO
#1 VARIANT

JAMAL CAMPBELL
#1 VARIANT

SKOTTIE YOUNG
#1 VARIANT